Tastes & Tales From Texas With Love

By

Peg Hein

D0534156

Copyright © 1984 by Peg Hein

Collaborator and Illustrator: Kathryn Lewis

Editor: Barbara Rodriguez

Revised Edition Editor: Mary T. Ullrich

Contributing Editors: Richard Zelade and Les Baker

Sixteenth Printing   July 1999

Title Design: Michael Earney

ISBN: 0-9613881-0-2

From Panhandle beef to Rio Grande grapefruit, from Big Bend beans to Big Thicket biscuits—these recipes reflect the variety, the uniqueness, and, we hope, the best of Lone Star State cooking. From Texas cooks who love to swap recipes we have accumulated a collection adopted and adapted through years of church suppers and potluck dinners, family feasts and famines, and countless kinds of Texas entertainings—from informal picnics and hoedowns to ultra-formal teas and dinner dances. In our search for Lone Star cookery, we have discovered new friends and long lost relatives and reached a better understanding of our state's roots and heritage. We have gathered, especially for you, recipes that range from gourmet to everyday, those that have been passed from generation to generation, and those so new their ingredients have only recently been added to the grocers' shelves. This book is a labor of love. From all who produced it, we give you now these

Tastes and Tales From Texas . . . With Love,

Peg Hein

CONTENTS

APPETIZERS

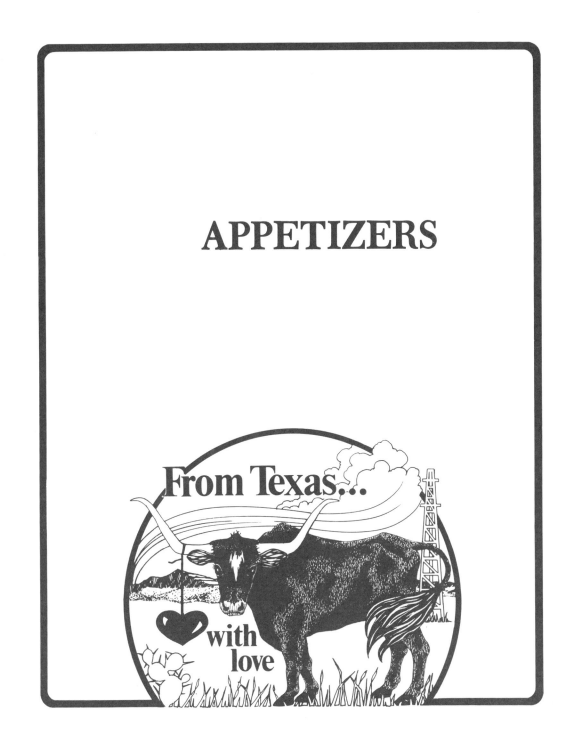

From Texas...
with love

NO, THE JALAPEÑO is not the state vegetable of Texas. But it is a versatile little critter, popping up fresh, pickled, stuffed, chicken-fried, jellied and in lollipops, jelly beans, and daiquiris. How about jalapeño wine? (No kidding, folks.) For those of you with delicate constitutions, the Aggies have developed a flameless jalapeño, but it has yet to catch fire on the open market.

Nachos

Yields 24 nachos

6 corn tortillas
Oil for frying tortillas
½ cup refried beans
¼ pound Monterrey Jack, Cheddar or Longhorn cheese, grated
Sliced pickled jalapeños to taste

Cut tortillas into quarters and fry in hot oil until crisp. Spread with refried beans, sprinkle with grated cheese and top with 2-3 slices jalapeño chiles. Broil until cheese melts. Guacamole and sour cream may be used to top nachos after broiling. Variations are limited only to your imagination. (If you're in a hurry, tortilla chips may be used to eliminate frying the tortillas.)

Jalapeño Cheese Squares

Yields 64 squares

4 cups Cheddar cheese, shredded
4 eggs beaten
1 teaspoon onion, minced
4 canned jalapeño peppers, seeded and chopped

Combine all ingredients and blend thoroughly. Spread mixture in an 8-inch pan. Bake at 350° for 30 minutes. Cut into 1-inch squares and serve hot.

Happy-tizers

These little tidbits are good without the jalapeños; but if you're making them for Texans, leave the chiles in.

Yields 36 appetizers

1 recipe for plain pastry
36 1-inch square slices Cheddar cheese
36 large pimento-stuffed olives
36 small slices jalapeño chiles

Roll out pastry on a lightly floured board or pastry cloth to 1/8-inch thickness and cut into 2½-inch squares. Place cheese in center of square and top with a slice of jalapeño and an olive. Bring two opposite corners of pastry over olive and pinch together. Repeat with other corners. Place on ungreased baking sheet and bake in preheated 450° oven for 10-15 minutes or until lightly browned.

Black-Eyed Pea Dip

Serves 12-14

1¾ cups dried black-eyed peas
5 canned jalapeño peppers, seeded and chopped (reserve liquid)
⅓ cup onion, chopped
1 clove garlic, minced
1 cup butter
2 cups shredded American cheese
1 4-ounce can chopped green chiles
1 tablespoon jalapeño pepper liquid

Wash and cook peas. Combine with jalapeño peppers, onion and garlic in blender container. Blend until smooth. Set aside. Combine butter and cheese in top of large double boiler. Cook and stir over low heat until melted. Add chiles, jalapeño liquid and pea mixture. Heat thoroughly and serve with corn chips. Tastes even better reheated.

Onion Mushroom Turnovers

Yields 35 appetizers

3 3-ounce packages cream cheese, softened
½ cup butter, softened
1½ cups flour
3 tablespoons butter
1 large onion, chopped fine
½ pound mushrooms, chopped fine
¼ teaspoon thyme
½ teaspoon salt
2 tablespoons flour
¼ cup sour cream

Blend cream cheese and butter. Add flour, mix well and refrigerate pastry at least 1 hour. Melt butter in a medium saucepan or skillet. Sauté onions and mushrooms until tender. Add seasonings and flour and stir in sour cream.

Roll chilled pastry 1/8-inch thick on pastry cloth or floured surface. Cut pastry in 3½-inch circles. Place scant teaspoon of filling in center of each circle and fold in half, sealing edges. Prick tops with fork. Bake at 450° for 15 minutes or until golden.

Texas Scramble

Yields 1½ quarts

1 12-ounce package oyster crackers
4 cups pretzel sticks
1 cup dry roasted peanuts
1 1-ounce package Hidden Valley Ranch Salad Dressing Mix
½ teaspoon garlic salt
1 teaspoon chili powder
½ cup oil

Mix dry ingredients together in large brown paper bag. Pour oil over top of dry ingredients and shake until well mixed.

Spread in large flat pan and bake at 200° for 1 hour.

Appetizers

ALTHOUGH TEXAS' SECOND largest city (and the nation's seventh biggest) was known as Dallas from its one-cabin beginning in 1841, it isn't known for whom it was named. Dallas County *WAS* named (in 1846) for U.S. Vice President (1845-49) George Mifflin Dallas, and the city also could have been named in his honor. Or it could have been named for the vice president's brother, Commodore A.J. of the U.S. Navy; or the brothers' father, U.S. Secretary of the Treasury Alexander James; or Joseph, a settler living near the new village in 1841; or James R., or Walter R., or Alexander Janes Dallas—brothers who served in the Army of the Republic of Texas.

Toasted Pecans

Yields 1 cup

1   cup pecans
2   tablespoons vinegar
1   tablespoon sugar
1   tablespoon melted butter

Measure pecans into a small bowl. Mix vinegar and sugar, pour over pecans and stir to coat thoroughly. Let stand for 15 minutes, stirring every 5 minutes. Place pecans in shallow baking dish and bake in 300° oven for 10 minutes. Add melted butter to pecans, stir and allow to bake for another 5 minutes.

"Big D" Pecans

Yields 2 cups

3   tablespoons butter or margarine
2   cups pecan halves
3   tablespoons Worcestershire sauce
1   teaspoon salt
½   teaspoon ground cinnamon
¼   teaspoon garlic powder
2-3 dashes Tabasco sauce

Melt butter in a 13x9-inch baking dish in 300° oven. Add pecans and stir until they are coated with butter. Bake for 15 minutes. Mix remaining ingredients, pour over pecans and stir gently until well mixed. Return to oven and bake another 15 minutes or until crisp.

Buffalo Wings

Buffalo Wings are proof that a good recipe can travel from New York to Texas in the minute it takes to make a phone call. These hot, spicy wings don't come from a bison, but originated in Buffalo, New York. Texas restaurants that have them on menus say they are becoming a favorite with customers. They may be served either as an appetizer or as a main dish.

Serves 10

3 pounds chicken wings
6 tablespoons Louisiana-style hot sauce
1 stick butter or margarine
Blue cheese dressing

Split wings at each joint. Discard tips (or save to use for broth). Put wing sections in baking dish and bake at 325° for 35 minutes. Place in bowl. Combine hot sauce and butter and pour over chicken wings. Cover and refrigerate at least 3 hours. Before serving, place wings in baking pan and bake at 425° for 10 minutes. Serve with blue cheese dressing for dipping.

Marinated Mushrooms

Yields 2 cups

1	pound small fresh mushrooms
2	tablespoons onion, chopped
⅔	cup wine vinegar
½	cup salad oil
2	garlic cloves, crushed
2	teaspoons sugar
½	teaspoon salt
6	whole peppercorns

Wipe mushrooms and remove stems. Place mushrooms in 1-quart bowl or jar. Combine remaining ingredients in a small saucepan, bring to a boil, lower heat and simmer 10 minutes. Pour hot mixture over mushrooms. Cool and refrigerate at least 24 hours before serving.

Mexican Five Layer Dip

Serves 8

2	10½-ounce cans bean dip
3	avocados, chopped
3	tablespoons lemon juice
8	ounces sour cream
½	cup salad dressing
½	package taco seasoning
3	medium tomatoes, chopped
4-6	green onions, chopped
1½	cups shredded sharp Cheddar cheese

Spread bean dip evenly on a 12-inch round tray. Mix avocados and lemon juice and spread over bean dip. Blend sour cream, salad dressing and taco seasoning and spread over avocados. Sprinkle tomatoes and green onions over sour cream mixture. Top with Cheddar cheese and garnish with ripe olives. Serve with tortilla or corn chips.

Appetizers

THE STRANGE SIGHT of camel caravans moving along the long "lower road" between San Antonio and El Paso both frightened and angered the Indians and ranchers of West Texas in the mid-1800's. This U.S. Army experiment to replace mules with camels was a temporary success because the camels could carry heavier loads, go without water for extended periods of time and survive by eating desert shrubs. The Civil War ended the experiment, and many of the camels were allowed to wander off into the hills of the Big Bend Country or were auctioned to the public by the federal government from Camp Verde, near Kerrville.

Big Bend Bean Dip

Yields 3 cups

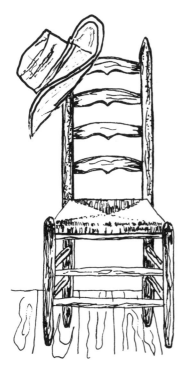

2 cups cooked pinto beans
2 tablespoons bacon drippings
 or butter
1 small onion, chopped
⅓ cup sharp cheese, grated
1 4-ounce can jalapeño chiles,
 drained, seeded and chopped
 Salt and pepper to taste

Mash beans until quite smooth, or blend in blender. Set aside. Sauté onion in bacon drippings or butter until soft. Add beans and remaining ingredients and stir over low heat until cheese melts. Serve warm with corn chips or tostados.

Hot Clam and Cheese Dip

Serves 8

1 small onion, finely chopped
½ green pepper, finely chopped
3 tablespoons butter
2 10-ounce cans minced clams, drained
¼ pound processed cheese, cubed
3 tablespoons catsup
1 tablespoon sherry
½ teaspoon cayenne pepper
1 tablespoon Worcestershire sauce

Sauté onion and green pepper in butter until tender. Add remaining ingredients and cook over very low heat or in top of double boiler until cheese melts, stirring often. Serve in chafing dish with assorted crackers.

Artichoke and Cheese Dip

Serves 8

1 14-ounce can artichoke hearts
1 6-ounce jar marinated artichoke hearts
1 4-ounce can green chiles
2 cups grated cheddar cheese
6 tablespoons mayonnaise

Drain artichoke hearts and green chiles and chop. Mix with remaining ingredients. Place in a 1½–quart casserole. Bake at 350° for 25-30 minutes or until warm. Serve with crackers.

Pattye's Green Chile Dip

This dip is not hot—just addictively good!

Serves 10

8 ounces cream cheese, softened
3 tablespoons mayonnaise
1 4-ounce can green chiles, diced
3 tablespoons onion, chopped
1 teaspoon lemon juice
Dash Worcestershire sauce
Paprika

Mix cream cheese and mayonnaise until blended. Add remaining ingredients and mix thoroughly. Refrigerate 3-4 hours, transfer to serving bowl, and sprinkle with paprika. Serve with corn or tortilla chips.

Commander's Shrimp Dip

From a marvelous cook and the wife of a retired Navy man who says she could rely on this recipe to be a success wherever they were stationed.

Serves 12

8 ounces cream cheese, softened
1 tablespoon curry powder
¼ teaspoon garlic powder
¼ cup chutney, minced
1 cup shrimp, cooked and diced
½ cup sour cream
2 tablespoons milk

Blend together cream cheese, curry powder, garlic powder and chutney. Mix sour cream and milk and add shrimp. Combine with cream cheese mixture. Mix thoroughly and refrigerate. Serve with crackers or chips.

Appetizers

THE TEXAS SESQUICENTENNIAL IN 1986 promises to be a full year of celebrations honoring 150 years of Texas independence. One event, the Texas Wagon Train, will involve more than 500,000 people on its journey to "Circle Texas for Past and Present." The Wagon Train will leave Sulphur Springs on January 2 and travel 2,800 miles, with overnight stays in 160 cities and towns, before arriving at the Fort Worth Stockyards on July 3. Thousands of people and families will get to join the Wagon Train as Trail Riders as the wagons roll through the state. Other festivities will include the Texas Independence Express Trains, a Hot Air Balloon Tour; art, dance, and theater performances; and enough other happenings to rival a World's Fair. It could turn out to be the biggest birthday party you'll ever see.

Sesquicentennial Spread

This wonderful dip is best when served in a hollowed-out round loaf of rye or pumpernickel bread.

Serves 14

1 10-ounce package frozen chopped spinach, thawed
2 tablespoons onion, minced
1 cup sour cream
1 cup mayonnaise
1 package Knorr's Swiss Vegetable Soup mix
1 5-ounce can water chestnuts, grated
1 round loaf *unsliced* rye or pumpernickel bread

Press thawed spinach to remove juice. Combine with remaining ingredients, except bread.

Slice 1 inch off top of bread. Use a grapefruit knife to hollow out bread loaf, leaving shell ½-inch thick to serve as container for dip. Tear or cut removed bread into chunks of suitable size for dunking.

This dip may be served with crackers or chips and still be a winner.

Appetizers

A TRAGIC FIGURE of Texas frontier days, Cynthia Ann Parker was abducted from the family stockade, Fort Parker, and taken into the Staked Plains in May 1836 by Comanches when she was 9 years old. Although there were reported glimpses of her through the years, all ransom efforts failed. She was taken as a wife by Peta Nocona, war chief of the Nokoni band, and bore him 3 children: Quanah, Pecos, and Topsanah. Recaptured by the Texas Rangers in 1860, Cynthia Ann could not adjust to the white world, and she starved herself to death. The half-white Quanah became head of the Plains Indians, leading them on many raids—and leading them finally, in defeat, to Oklahoma Territory reservations. From there, he represented his people most ably with Washington leaders. The last chief of the Comanches died in 1911.

Chili Cheese Log

Chili powder gives the cheese a pleasant spiciness.

Serves 8

½ pound Monterrey Jack cheese, shredded
1 tablespoon onion, minced
6 pimento stuffed olives, chopped
¼ cup mayonnaise
½ cup saltine cracker crumbs, finely crushed
2 tablespoons chili powder

Combine cheese, onion, olives and mayonnaise. Mix well. Add 2 tablespoons cracker crumbs and blend well. Form mixture into a 6-inch roll. Mix chili powder and remaining cracker crumbs; roll log in chili mixture until thoroughly coated. Serve with crackers.

THE LAST INDIAN battle in Texas was fought in Palo Duro Canyon in 1874, when Colonel Ranald MacKenzie and his raiders attacked a huge encampment of Kiowa, Cheyenne, Comanche and Arapaho. The raiders destroyed over 100 lodges and 1,400 horses and mules and drove the surviving Indians to an Oklahoma Territory reservation. Today, Palo Duro Canyon is the setting for the spectacular outdoor drama *TEXAS* in which Texas history is reenacted using the beautiful canyon wall and rim as a backdrop.

Canyon Mustard Cheese Spread

The men raved about this spread at one of our tasting parties.

Yields 2½ cups

1 tablespoon butter, melted
1 cup pecans, finely chopped
2 tablespoons prepared mustard
8 ounces Cheddar or American cheese, shredded
3 ounces cream cheese, softened
2 tablespoons Worcestershire sauce
1 teaspoon Durkee's dressing
2 tablespoons butter, melted

Combine melted butter and pecans in large, flat pan and roast at 200° for about 1 hour. Stir occasionally; do not allow to brown. Combine remaining ingredients and blend thoroughly. Add toasted pecans and mix. This may be used as a spread for crackers or a dip for fresh vegetables.

PECAN SHELLING was a pioneer industry in Texas, but Gustav Duerler of San Antonio turned it into a big business. After serving in the Confederate Army, Duerler established a candy factory and later a pecan-shelling business, with his shellers cracking the nuts with railroad spikes. By 1882 production had outstripped local demand, so Duerler started shipping pecan meats back east. He began using mechanical crackers in 1889 and bought the world's first power-driven cracker in 1914.

Hot Pecan Spread

Serves 8

1 8-ounce package cream cheese, softened
2 tablespoons milk
2 ounces dried beef, chopped
¼ cup green pepper, minced
2 tablespoons onion, minced
½ cup sour cream
½ teaspoon garlic salt
¼ teaspoon pepper

Topping
2 tablespoons butter
½ teaspoon salt
½ cup pecans, chopped

Blend together cheese and milk. Stir in dried beef, green pepper, onion, sour cream and seasoning. Mix well and pour into 1-quart baking casserole.

To make topping, melt butter in a small skillet. Add salt and pecans and saute over medium heat until lightly browned. Spread over cream cheese mixture and bake at 350° for 20 minutes. Serve hot with wheat crackers.

BACK IN 1937 the citizens of Crystal City, 45 miles from the Rio Grande in the heart of the Texas Winter Garden area, erected a statue of Popeye the Sailor Man. Since then he has proudly attested to the many virtues of spinach. Some say the statue was erected to help offset "anti-spinach calumny" in the New Yorker magazine: a cartoon depicting a youngster who, upon being told the vegetable was broccoli, replied, "I say it's spinach and I say the hell with it!"

Special Spinach Spread

Here's a delicious spread or dip that is very low in calories.

Yields 1 cup

1 10-ounce package frozen spinach, thawed
2 tablespoons minced green onions
¼ cup yogurt
½ teaspoon lemon juice
½ teaspoon Worcestershire sauce
½ teaspoon horseradish
4 drops hot pepper sauce

Squeeze spinach to remove juice. Combine remaining ingredients and mix with spinach. Cover and refrigerate for several hours.

Serve with whole wheat crackers.

Cheese and Ripe Olive Spread

This spread can be served cold as a spread for crackers, but when it's spread on slices of party rye bread and toasted in the oven the blended flavors are marvelous.

Yields 1½ cups

3 ounces Cheddar cheese, shredded
3 tablespoons chopped ripe olives
½ cup green onion, chopped fine
½ cup mayonnaise
½ teaspoon curry powder
Party rye bread

Mix all ingredients except bread and refrigerate for several hours. Spread on slices of bread and bake at 400° for 3-4 minutes.

HISTORIC DEL RIO is called the "Queen City of the Rio Grande." A raid by the Kickapoo Indians caused an early rancher's cattle to scatter, and search for the missing cows led to discovery of the San Felipe Springs, site of the modern city. The fascinating history of the area is captured by the Whitehead Memorial Museum, which is made up of several buildings and includes a pioneer log cabin, an old shepherd's wagon and the grave of Judge Roy Bean, the only "Law West of the Pecos."

Whitehead Museum Hot Hamburger

This Mexican paté has been a tradition at Del Rio fiestas for generations. The family recipes for Hot Hamburger are closely guarded secrets; but this one from Estella Munoz, Director of the Whitehead Museum, was the result of experimenting, testing and tasting.

Yields 6 cups

1 pound lean ground beef, raw
4 ounces cooked ham, chopped
1 cup celery, chopped
⅓ pound Cheddar cheese
1 small onion, chopped
1 apple, peeled, cored
 and chopped
40 saltine crackers, crumbled
2 lemons, juice and pulp
 Salt and pepper to taste

Mix all ingredients together and put through a food processor, blender or, best of all, a meat grinder to make a paté. Blend in any good hot sauce slowly until desired degree of hotness is reached.

BREADS AND BREAKFAST

From Texas....

with love

Breads and Breakfast

THE DALLAS COWBOYS have captured the hearts and enthusiasm of Texans and sports enthusiasts throughout the entire nation. "America's Team" has thrilled fans with a score of straight winning seasons, 5 trips to the Super Bowl and 2 World Championships. Founded in 1960 as the Dallas Rangers, they were soon renamed the Dallas Cowboys. Like the bluebonnet, oil derrick and longhorn, the silver, blue and white Cowboys helmet has become another symbol of Texas.

Bob Breunig's Apple Bread

This good apple bread recipe comes from Bob Breunig, a noted middle linebacker for the Dallas Cowboys.

Yields 2 loaves

1 cup oil
1 cup sugar
3 eggs
2 cups apples, chopped
2 teaspoons vanilla
3 cups flour (unbleached)
1 teaspoon soda
¼ teaspoon salt
1 cup nuts, chopped

Mix oil, sugar, eggs, apples and vanilla. Combine dry ingredients and add to sugar mixture. Add nuts and mix thoroughly. Pour into 2 small ungreased loaf pans. Bake at 350° for 1 hour. Cool for 10 minutes before removing from pans. Serve hot with butter.

Dill Toasts

These crisp little toasts may be used for spreads, dips, soups, salads or just plain munching. They keep well in an airtight container.

Yield 40 slices

½ cup butter, softened
1 clove garlic, minced
½ teaspoon onion salt
¼ teaspoon celery salt
20 slices very thin white bread
Dill weed and seasoned salt to taste

Mix butter, garlic, onion salt and celery salt together and spread on bread. Sprinkle dill weed and seasoning salt on butter to taste. Cut slices in half. Toast in a 225° oven for 1½-2 hours or until very crisp and lightly browned.

Port Neches Bread

Serves 8

1 loaf French bread
¼ pound margarine
½ cup mayonnaise
1 tablespoon green onion, chopped
¾ cup black olives, chopped
4 ounces Monterrey Jack cheese, shredded

Slice French bread in half lengthways. Melt margarine in a small pan over low heat. Add mayonnaise and blend with a wire whisk. Add remaining ingredients and mix well. Spread margarine mixture on cut sides of bread and wrap each half individually in foil. Refrigerate overnight. When ready to use, preheat oven to 350° and bake for 15-20 minutes. Slice diagonally into 2-inch slices.

Breads and Breakfast

A WHITE BUFFALO is a rare sight these days—and always has been. Folks in the Panhandle town of Snyder built a statue honoring the last albino bison killed up their way at the tail end of the Great American Buffalo Slaughter over 100 years ago. Kiowa Indian legend decrees that one day a white buffalo will lead a herd as big as the original one (60 million head, that is) out of a Panhandle cave, ready to reclaim Texas and the rest of the Great Plains.

Freezer Bran Bread

This bread from Snyder has an extraordinarily good flavor. Since the dough freezes well, you can thaw, let rise and bake whenever you want.

Yields 3 loaves

9½ cups flour, unsifted
3 cups whole bran cereal
   or bran flakes
¼ cup sugar
4 teaspoons salt
3 packages dry yeast
½ cup margarine
3 cups hot water (120-130°)
⅓ cup dark molasses
   Melted margarine

Combine 2 cups flour, bran, sugar, salt and yeast. Add margarine, water and molasses. Beat 2 minutes at medium speed. Add 1 cup flour and beat 2 minutes at high speed. Continue to add flour to make a stiff dough. Turn out onto floured surface; knead until smooth and elastic. Cover and let rest 15 minutes.

Roll and divide into 3 equal loaves; brush tops with margarine. Place on greased baking sheet, cover tightly with plastic wrap; freeze. When frozen, place in plastic airtight bag. Keeps frozen up to 4 weeks.

Remove from freezer 5½ hours before baking. Thaw 2½ hours; shape into 6-inch round loaves. Place on greased baking sheet and let rise until doubled in size. Bake at 350° for 40-45 minutes.

Breads and Breakfast

FAYETTEVILLE, a tiny hamlet known in the early 1800's for its barbecues and town feasts, attracted so many visitors to such events that the food supply would run out. Latecomers were told they'd simply have to "lick the skillet," and thus the town became known as Lickskillet.

Lickskillet Inn Beer Bread

Jeanette Donaldson, owner of the Lickskillet Bed and Breakfast Inn, prepares this loaf, the Texas version of a continental breakfast, for her guests.

Yields 1 loaf

3 cups self-rising flour
1 tablespoon sugar
1 beer, room temperature
  (best if never chilled)

Combine dry ingredients. Add beer and mix to make soft dough. Turn out into a greased 8x4½-inch loaf pan. Set aside 15 minutes to rise. Bake at 375° for 40 minutes or until brown.

This bread slices best when cold; or may be torn apart and eaten hot with butter. It's delicious toasted and served with preserves.

Note: The Lickskillet Inn uses Martha White's Hot-Rise Flour and Shiner Beer. However, if these products are not available, the recipe will still work.

Breads and Breakfast

THE MEXICAN PEOPLE are friendly and gracious to visitors; Texans are equally pleased to play the host, and crossing the Rio Grande is easy and simple. But the citizens of the most frequently used crossing of the entire U.S.-Mexican border between Laredo and Nuevo Laredo were once not as accommodating. In 1839, they declared they were the Republic of the Rio Grande and would not bow to either nation. They kept their vow for two years, even launching a military effort toward the interior of Mexico.

Mexican Bolillos

These wonderful crusty rolls are served with every meal in Mexico—and no wonder!

Yields 24 rolls

1 package dry yeast
2 teaspoons sugar
2 cups warm water
2 teaspoons salt
6 cups flour

Combine yeast, sugar and warm water and stir until dissolved. Add salt and two cups flour and mix thoroughly. Add remaining flour, 1 cup at a time, mixing with each addition.

Turn out dough on a lightly floured surface and knead until smooth and satiny. Place dough in a greased bowl, turn to grease top and cover with a towel. Let rise in a warm place until doubled in bulk. Punch dough down and divide into slender rolls about 3 inches long; twist each end. Place bolillos on a greased cookie sheet and allow to double in bulk. Lightly oil tops of rolls, slash top with a sharp knife and bake at 400° for 10 minutes. Reduce heat to 350°, bake another 20 minutes or until golden brown. Serve hot with lots of butter.

BREAD AND COUNTRY-WESTERN music went together like bread and butter at one time in Texas. One of the original western swing bands, the Lightcrust Doughboys, premiered in 1931 on Fort Worth radio station WBAP, singing the praises of Burris Mills' popular Lightcrust flour and featuring such musical legends as Bob Wills, Sleepy Johnson, Milton Brown and Leon McAuliffe. The Lightcrust Doughboys were the brainchild of W. Lee "Pappy" O'Daniel, who later started his own flour company and hired his own band, The Hillbilly Boys, to hawk his product. The Hillbilly Boys figured prominently in O'Daniel's successful 1938 campaign for governor.

Orange Date Pecan Bread

Yields 1 loaf

½   cup butter
¼   cup sugar
½   cup light brown sugar
2   eggs, beaten
4   teaspoons orange peel, grated
½   teaspoon vanilla
½   cup sour cream
½   cup orange juice
2½ cups flour
1   teaspoon baking powder
1   teaspoon soda
½   teaspoon salt
1   cup dates, chopped
½   cup pecans, chopped

Cream butter and sugars in large mixing bowl. Add eggs, orange peel and vanilla and beat until light and fluffy. Add sour cream and orange juice and beat thoroughly. Sift flour, baking powder, soda and salt. Add to creamed mixture and stir until blended. Fold in dates and pecans and pour into greased 9x5-inch loaf pan. Bake at 350° for 60-70 minutes or until bread tests done. Allow to cool in pan for 10 minutes, remove and cool on a rack. Serve with cream cheese.

Breads and Breakfast

THE YELLOW ROSE OF TEXAS is a rousing, unofficial Texas song that seldom fails to liven up a gathering of Texans. No one knows who wrote the song, but it is a tribute to the beautiful young mulatto who was the heroine of the battle of San Jacinto. According to legend, Santa Anna was so preoccupied with the charms of the captured young servant girl, Emily Morgan, that he failed miserably as commander of the Mexican Army. The unprepared Mexican troops were so overwhelmed by Sam Houston and his volunteer army of Texians that the battle lasted only 18 minutes. The Battle of San Jacinto ended the Texas Revolution and made Texas an independent nation.

Skillet Cheddar Cornbread

Serves 10-12

1 cup yellow cornmeal
1 cup all-purpose flour
2 tablespoons sugar
1 tablespoon baking powder
1 teaspoon salt
1 cup milk
2 eggs, beaten
2 cups Cheddar cheese, shredded

Combine cornmeal, flour, sugar, baking powder and salt in a large mixing bowl. Set aside. Combine milk, eggs and cheese and add to dry ingredients. Mix thoroughly. Pour batter into hot, greased 10-inch iron skillet. Bake at 425° for 15 minutes or until cornbread is golden.

Breads and Breakfast

THE OLD BAKERY, built on Austin's Congress Avenue in 1876 by Swedish immigrant Charles Lundberg, was saved from demolition and partially restored in 1963 by combined efforts of the Austin Heritage Society and the Austin Junior League. It later became a co-sponsored project of the Austin Parks and Recreation Department and the First Lady's Volunteer Program. A visit to this landmark, with its Confectionery of wonderful breads, pastries and other goodies, offers a true taste of Austin hospitality.

Swedish Rye Bread

This comes from a lady who baked for the Old Bakery for several years.

Yields 6 loaves

2 packages dry yeast
1 tablespoon sugar
5 cups lukewarm water
13-14 cups sifted flour
4 teaspoons salt
1 cup sugar
1 12-ounce jar molasses
⅔ cup shortening or bacon drippings
2 cups sifted rye flour

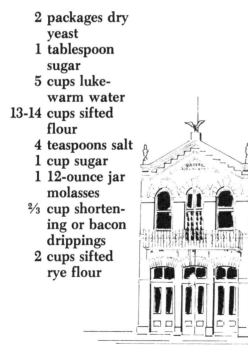

In a large bowl dissolve yeast and 1 tablespoon sugar in 1 cup lukewarm water. Add the remaining 4 cups water and 5 cups sifted flour. Mix thoroughly, and let stand until dough begins to bubble, approximately 1½ hours.

Add salt, 1 cup sugar, shortening, molasses and rye flour. Mix well. Add remaining flour to make a soft ball. Turn out on floured surface and knead until dough is smooth and satiny (about 10 minutes). Place back in the bowl, cover and let rise in a warm place until doubled in bulk.

Knead briefly, form into 6 loaves and place in greased 8x4½-inch loaf pans. Let rise again until doubled in bulk. Bake at 300° for 1 hour or until done.

THE TEXAS STATE FAIR is the largest and most spectacular annual state fair in the nation. It features a Broadway musical, a major rodeo competition, the annual classic football contest between the University of Oklahoma and the University of Texas and dozens of other enticing events as lively and varied as the state itself. Ribbons of all colors are awarded for the best livestock, produce, talent and special skills. Champion cooks from all over Texas bring their specialties to be judged in a mouthwatering display of culinary talent.

Becky's Blueberry Buttermilk Biscuits

These muffins won both a Blue Ribbon and Best of Show award in the 1983 Texas State Fair. Becky's husband, Sam Higgins, is author of the cookbook I'm Glad I Ate When I Did, 'Cause I'm Not Hungry Now, which features down-home, country style cooking.

Yields 1½ dozen

2 cups sifted flour
½ cup sugar
3 teaspoons baking powder
¼ teaspoon baking soda
1 teaspoon salt
⅓ cup Crisco shortening
1 teaspoon grated orange peel
1 egg, beaten
¾ cup buttermilk
½ cup *frozen* blueberries (must be frozen blueberries)

Topping
2-3 tablespoons butter, melted
3 tablespoons sugar
¼ teaspoon cinnamon
Dash of nutmeg

Preheat oven to 400°. Combine first 5 ingredients. Cut in Crisco until mixture resembles coarse meal. Add orange peel; mix lightly. Combine egg and buttermilk; add to flour mixture, stirring to blend. Add frozen blueberries and stir gently. Transfer dough to a lightly floured surface. Knead gently 5 or 6 times. Pat dough to ½-inch thickness. Cut out biscuits with floured 2-inch cutter. Bake on ungreased cookie sheet 15 minutes or until brown.

Combine topping ingredients and brush on top of biscuits while warm.

Breads and Breakfast

SCHULENBURG IS MORE than just the home of some of the best wurst in Texas, it's also the hometown of Gus Baumgarten, the man who revolutionized baking in America. Originally a cottonseed oil miller, Baumgarten invented a cottonseed flour; and future President Herbert Hoover sent government chemists to Schulenburg in 1917 to research it. While the chemists studied, Baumgarten fiddled around with a thermometer in his home oven and invented controlled-heat baking in the process. Hearing of Baumgarten's revolutionary baking method, President Hoover asked him to instruct the government's corps of home economists in this new cooking technique. The result was a thermostat on almost every oven subsequently produced in America.

Biscuit and Sausage Rolls

Serves 4

1 10-ounce can refrigerated biscuits
½ pound pork sausage
1 tablespoon onion, chopped
¼ cup apple, chopped fine

½ tablespoon brown sugar
¼ teaspoon cinnamon
1 cup Cheddar cheese, grated

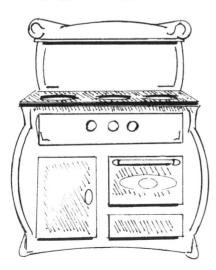

Place biscuits on a floured surface in 3 rows of 3 each. Use extra biscuit to fill in spaces between biscuits as you pat and roll until seams are joined to make a square of pastry. Crumble sausage in a medium skillet; add onion and cook until sausage is no longer pink. Drain and spread evenly over biscuit dough. Mix apple, brown sugar and cinnamon and sprinkle over sausage. Top with cheese. Carefully roll up dough and filling and cut into 8 slices. Place slices flat in sections of a muffin tin. Bake at 400° for 12-15 minutes or until cheese is bubbly and biscuits are lightly browned.

Breads and Breakfast

EVEN THE GREATEST inventor can come up with a colossal clinker—take Gail Borden, Jr.'s, meat biscuit. Borden boiled Texas beef down to an extract, mixed it with flour and baked it to create a portable dehydrated biscuit. Just add water, heat and eat. The biscuit won several prizes at international exhibitions in the 1850's. Borden deemed it perfect for armies on the march and promoted it worldwide. But most who ate it vowed to go hungry next time, and so the meat biscuit marched into oblivion. Never mind—Borden's evaporated milk process made the soldier, surveyor, stockman, publisher, public servant, philanthropist, entrepreneur and inventor a very rich man.

Buttermilk Biscuits

These old-fashioned drop biscuits are hard to stop eating.

Yields 20 biscuits

2 cups flour, sifted
1 tablespoon baking powder
¾ teaspoon salt
½ teaspoon soda
½ teaspoon cream of tartar
¼ cup shortening
1 cup buttermilk
6 tablespoons butter

Sift dry ingredients together into mixing bowl. Cut in shortening until blended. Add buttermilk and mix well. Drop by tablespoon onto a greased baking sheet. Put a thin pat of butter on top of each biscuit. Bake at 450° for 10 minutes.

Sesame Seed Buttermilk Biscuits

Using basic recipe for Buttermilk Biscuits, roll dough ½-inch thick on a lightly floured surface. Cut with a 2-inch biscuit cutter or juice glass. Place biscuits on a greased baking sheet, top each with a thin pat of butter and ¼ teaspoon sprinkling of sesame seeds.

Cheese Chalet Muffins

The Cheese Chalet in Lampasas specializes in good cheese and in food prepared with cheese. These muffins, with a touch of dill and mustard, are a popular selection from its menu.

Yields 16 muffins

1½ cups yellow cornmeal
1½ cups Bisquick
1 tablespoon baking powder
1 tablespoon dry dill weed
1 tablespoon dry mustard
1 tablespoon sugar
1 egg
1 tablespoon oil
1¼ cups milk
1 cup Cojack cheese, grated (Cojack is a blend of Colby, Longhorn and Monterrey Jack)

If you have a food processor, combine all ingredients and blend slowly.

Otherwise, combine dry ingredients in a large mixing bowl. Add egg, milk and corn oil and mix until dry ingredients are moistened. Add cheese and blend thoroughly, using an electric mixer at low speed. Spoon into greased muffin cups. Bake at 350° for 30 minutes.

Hush Puppies

Yields 1 dozen hush puppies

1 cup cornmeal
½ cup flour
1 teaspoon baking powder
½ teaspoon soda
1 teaspoon salt
1 teaspoon sugar
¼ cup onion, finely chopped
1 cup buttermilk
1 egg, beaten
Oil or shortening

Combine cornmeal, flour, baking powder, soda, salt and sugar in medium mixing bowl. Mix onion, buttermilk and egg. Add to cornmeal mixture and stir until blended. Heat 1 inch of oil or shortening in heavy skillet to 375°. Drop batter by spoonfuls into hot grease and fry until golden brown. Drain and serve.

Breads and Breakfast

BEFORE THE ADVENT of large-scale irrigation, Americans called the Texas High Plains the Great American Desert, a place where even a jackrabbit would be well advised to pack a lunch. With the turn of the century and the increasing use of water wells and pumps, Albert Hinn became one of the first to recognize the region's vast wheat-growing capabilities. Shortly after moving to Plainview and entering the real estate business, Hinn bought the Harvest Queen Flour Mill and developed it into one of Texas' major mills. He also developed new flours and introduced experimental varieties of wheat to local farms.

Karen's Peach Muffins

Yields 1½ dozen muffins

2 cups flour
½ cup sugar
2 teaspoons baking powder
½ teaspoon baking soda
½ teaspoon salt
½ teaspoon ground cinnamon
½ teaspoon ground nutmeg
  Dash ground mace
1 egg, beaten
⅓ cup vegetable oil
⅓ cup milk
1 8-ounce carton peach yogurt
½ cup dried peaches, finely chopped
2 tablespoons flour
2 tablespoons brown sugar
2 tablespoons pecans, chopped
½ teaspoon ground cinnamon
2 tablespoons soft butter

Combine first eight ingredients in a large bowl. Mix egg, oil, milk, yogurt and dried peaches. Add to dry ingredients, stirring only enough to moisten. Fill greased muffin tins ⅔ full.

Combine 2 tablespoons flour, brown sugar, pecans and ½ teaspoon cinnamon in small bowl. Cut butter into flour mixture until it resembles coarse meal. Sprinkle 1 teaspoon of mixture over top of each muffin. Bake at 400° for 20 minutes or until golden.

Breads and Breakfast

LADY BIRD JOHNSON gives much of her time and incredible energy to the National Wildflower Research Center, which she founded. The twofold purpose of the Center, located near Austin, is to study the thousands of wildflower species in the United States and to act as a national clearinghouse for anyone with questions or information about them. Mrs. Johnson is doing her best to ensure that others will always be able to enjoy the wildflowers that she says have "enriched my life and fed my soul."

Lady Bird's Popovers

Yields 5-6 popovers

1 cup flour, sifted
¼ teaspoon salt
2 eggs, beaten

1 cup milk
2 tablespoons shortening, melted

Sift flour and salt together. Combine eggs, milk and shortening and gradually add to flour mixture. Beat about 1 minute or until batter is smooth. Fill greased, sizzling-hot popover pans ¾ full and bake in a very hot over (450°) for 20 minutes. Reduce heat to 350° and continue baking for 15-20 minutes.

Note: If you do not have popover pans, ovenproof custard cups may be used.

Breads and Breakfast

"SEGUIN, Home of the World's Largest Pecan," is inscribed over a large replica of Texas' favorite nut adorning the courthouse square in Seguin. Another nut figured in the early days of the town, which was originally called Walnut Springs. However, the name was soon changed to Seguin as a tribute to Juan Seguin, who served with Sam Houston in the Texas battle for independence and who later became mayor of San Antonio and a Texas state senator.

Cranberry-Pecan Coffee Cake

Serves 12

¾ cup butter, softened
1½ cups sugar
3 eggs
3 cups flour
1½ teaspoons baking powder
1½ teaspoons soda
¾ teaspoon salt
1½ cups sour cream
1½ teaspoons almond extract
1 16-ounce can whole-berry cranberry sauce
¾ cup pecans, chopped

Cream butter and sugar in mixing bowl. Add eggs, 1 at a time, beating after each addition. Combine flour, baking powder, soda and salt, and add alternately with sour cream. Add almond extract and mix. Pour half the batter into a greased 10-inch tube pan. Spread cranberry sauce and pecans over batter. Add remaining batter and bake at 375° for 1 hour or until cake tests done. Allow to cool 5 minutes before removing from pan.

Glaze:
1 cup confectioners sugar
1-2 tablespoons hot water
¾ teaspoon almond extract

Sift confectioners sugar in mixing bowl. Add water until glaze is of desired consistency. Stir in almond extract and spread over cake while still warm.

Breads and Breakfast

THE ALAMO—the most revered of Texas shrines—has, in fact, spent much of its life as a stepchild. Originally built as a chapel for the Mission San Antonio de Valero, the Alamo and the rest of the mission stood abandoned by 1793. Spanish soldiers barracked there during Mexico's War for Independence; and it wasn't until then that the ex-mission came to be called the Alamo, perhaps because of the *alamo* (cottonwood) trees growing nearby. Mexican soldiers occupied the Alamo from 1821 until the Texians captured it from them in 1835. After that time the Alamo fell into near ruin. Ownership and use of what was left of the shrine bounced around for the next 50 years, until the state bought the chapel and gave custody of it to the Daughters of the Republic of Texas, who have faithfully cared for the Alamo ever since.

Heroes' Scrapple

Serves 8

2 pounds pork, boiled until tender (reserve broth)
1 quart pork broth
1½ cups cornmeal
2 cups cold water
1 teaspoon salt
½ teaspoon garlic salt

Trim pork, discard fat and bones and shred meat. Bring pork broth to boil in 3-quart saucepan. Mix cornmeal and cold water, and stir into boiling broth. Cook and stir until mixture begins to thicken. Add meat and seasonings. Cook over low heat for 20 minutes. Pour into greased loaf pan and cool. When set, slice and fry in hot oil. Serve with syrup or molasses.

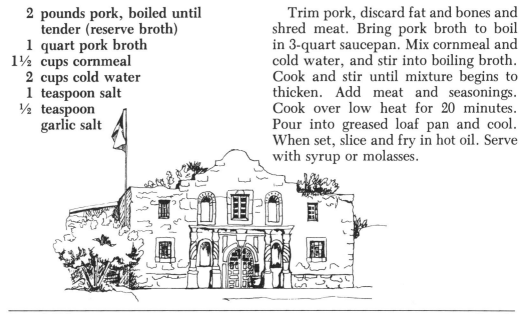

Breads and Breakfast

THE SIZE OF TEXAS RANCHES boggles the minds of non-Texans and city folk. Ranches have to be large because most are in arid south and west Texas where several acres of grassland are necessary to sustain one cow. Today, while ranching in Texas is big business and many ranches are incorporated, the word ranch still conjures up images of cowboys, bunkhouses, horses, saddles and branding irons, rather than businessmen and board rooms. The ranching heritage remains basic to the uniqueness of Texas.

Huevos Rancheros

You don't have to live on a ranch to enjoy a leisurely breakfast of eggs poached in a sauce of green chiles and tomatoes, heaped on a corn tortilla and topped with bubbling cheese.

Serves 4

1 tablespoon bacon drippings
1 small onion, chopped
2 cups canned stewed tomatoes
1 4-ounce can green chiles, chopped, undrained
½ teaspoon salt
½ cup oil
4 corn tortillas
4 eggs
1 cup Monterrey Jack cheese, grated

Heat bacon drippings in a 10-inch skillet. Sauté onion until soft. Add stewed tomatoes, green chiles and salt. Simmer until liquid is reduced by half. Heat oil in a small skillet and soften tortillas by dipping briefly in oil. Drain tortillas and cover to keep warm. Drop eggs, evenly spaced, into sauce and cook 3 minutes. Cover pan and cook another minute. Place warm tortillas on an ovenproof plate, top with eggs surrounded by sauce and sprinkle with cheese. Slide under broiler until cheese melts.

Breads and Breakfast

THE MASSES OF BLUEBONNETS along the highways and byways of Texas delight anyone lucky enough to view them. Quick thinking by members of the Texas Chapter of Colonial Dames, who nominated the blossom for state flower before it was widely known, led to its selection as Texas' No. 1 bloom. Several possibilities were being debated by the 1901 State House of Representatives when "Cactus Jack" Garner made an eloquent and impassioned plea for his favorite, the cactus flower. Colonial Dames present in the House Chamber, sensing defeat of their favorite, quickly countered with a painting of bluebonnets, which some of the legislators had never seen. As they unveiled the picture, the House erupted in loud applause; and the bluebonnet became the official state flower by unanimous vote.

Nelle's Nopalitos con Huevos

Nopalitos, the tender young leaves of the cactus plant, are a favorite food in southern and western parts of Texas. They are sold fresh in some Texas grocery stores, but are more widely available in cans or jars. They add a distinctive touch to salads, eggs and meats.

Serves 4

1 8-ounce can nopalitos
3 tablespoons butter
2 tablespoons light cream
8 eggs, slightly beaten
    Salt and pepper to taste

Rinse nopalitos thoroughly and drain or pat dry. Melt butter in large skillet, add nopalitos and sauté gently for about 2 minutes. Add cream to eggs, season with salt and pepper and pour over nopalitos. Scramble over low heat until barely set. Serve with sausage and fruit.

Breads and Breakfast

BOOKS WRITTEN in the mid-1800's assured potential investors that there was not the slightest element of uncertainty in raising cattle on the plains of Texas. Despite such Pollyanna assurances cattle prices plummeted by 75 percent within the next few years and ranchers suffered a series of wretched blizzards, droughts and grasshopper invasions. Such disasters, along with the coming of windmills and steam-powered engines, resulted in the division of many of the great cattle ranches into farms. Soon farming replaced ranching as the Panhandle's prime business.

Decimae's Ham and Swiss Cheese Brotchen

This recipe comes from a fine Panhandle cook who enjoys serving it for breakfast or brunch.

Serves 6

3 English muffins, split
3 tablespoons butter, softened
12 ounces Swiss cheese
6 slices ham, smoked or boiled
3 eggs, beaten
2 cups milk
1 teaspoon salt
¼ teaspoon pepper

Spread English muffin halves with butter and place split side up in 13x9-inch baking dish. Slice half the cheese and divide between muffins. Cover cheese with ham slices. Mix eggs, milk, salt and pepper and pour over open-faced sandwiches. Grate reserved cheese and sprinkle on top of egg mixture. Refrigerate several hours or overnight. When ready to bake, preheat oven to 350° and bake for 40 minutes. Egg mixture should be set but not dry.

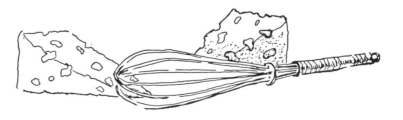

SOUPS AND SALADS

From Texas...

with love

Soups and Salads

THE TEXAS RANGER chapter of Texas history is filled with more drama and braver heroes than a top fiction writer could invent. Formed in 1835 by Stephen F. Austin, the Rangers were charged with the protection of west and south Texas settlers from hostile Indians. Later they took on Mexican bandits, fence-cutting ranchers and countless outlaws. Their territory was vast, their job dangerous and their pay low, yet this small band of men did their job with courage, steadiness and confidence. Their legend is brought to life in the Texas Ranger Museum and Hall of Fame located at Fort Fisher in Waco.

Ranger Nine-Bean Soup

Parcels of mixed pinto, black, northern, red and tiny lima beans with split peas are available at many food stores. The interesting combination of flavors makes a good soup.

Serves 6-8

1   pound mixed beans
2   quarts water
    Ham hocks or ham bone
1   large onion
1   clove garlic, mashed
1   teaspoon chili powder
1   28-ounce can tomatoes
    Juice of 1 lemon
    Salt and pepper

Wash beans thoroughly and place in large kettle. Cover with water and soak overnight. Drain. Add water, ham hocks or ham bone and onion. Simmer 2 hours. Remove meat from bones and return to beans. Add spices, tomatoes and lemon juice. Simmer another hour to blend flavors. Salt and pepper to taste. Serve with cornbread.

Soups and Salads

CORN IS THE OLDEST cultivated crop in Texas. The Caddo Indians were growing it when the Spanish first wandered into East Texas in the late 1600's. Corn is the easiest of the grain crops to grow, harvest and prepare—factors which made it perfect for frontier life. Early settlers toasted, boiled, fried and dried their young corn. Mature corn was ground into meal and, with the addition of water, salt and a good fire, it became mush, ashcake, johnnycake, hoecake, pone dodgers or tamales. Sugar, yeast, eggs, spices and soda were welcome, but unnecessary, additions. Cheap and nutritious corn was the staff of life for many early colonists.

Manuel's Sopa de Elote (Sweet Corn Soup)

Manuel's Cafe y Bar on Congress Avenue in Austin specializes in food from central Mexico, and their corn soup brings raves from everyone who tastes it. The poblano peppers, cilantro and cheese lift it above the ordinary.

Serves 8-10

¼ cup butter
¼ medium white onion, cut into narrow strips
1 medium poblano pepper, toasted, peeled and cut into narrow strips
8 cups corn kernels, pureed in blender or food processor
1 quart half-and half
1 quart milk
1 large sprig cilantro, minced
Salt to taste
1 cup Monterrey Jack cheese, grated

Melt butter in 6-quart saucepan; add onion, pepper and corn. Sauté 3 minutes over high heat, stirring constantly. Add half-and-half, milk and cilantro. Salt to taste. Heat to boiling point; immediately reduce heat and hold soup at a low simmer for 10 minutes. Ladle into bowls and sprinkle with cheese. ¡Buen provecho!

Chilled Cucumber Soup

A soup for a summer day! The touch of dill with the smooth, creamy cucumber base is wonderful.

Serves 8

2 large cucumbers
½ cup onion, chopped fine
3 cups chicken stock
1 cup sour cream
¼ teaspoon dry mustard
½ teaspoon fresh dill or
    ¼ teaspoon dill weed
    Salt and pepper to taste
    Chopped chives for garnish

Peel one cucumber, slice lengthwise, remove seeds and chop. Place chopped cucumber, onion and two cups chicken stock in medium saucepan and simmer for 15 minutes. Pureé in blender or food processor. Peel second cucumber, remove seeds and grate coarsely. Add this with sour cream, remaining cup of chicken stock, and seasonings to the puree. Chill thoroughly. Serve in glass bowls or mugs garnished with chopped chives.

Texas Avocado Soup

Serves 6

2 large ripe avocados
½ teaspoon salt
    Dash of white pepper
2 cups chicken broth
⅓ cup dry Sherry
1 cup heavy cream
    Thin avocado slices or
    sour cream for garnish

Peel avocado and cut into chunks. Pureé avocados, salt, pepper, chicken broth and sherry in blender or food processor. Stir in cream and chill well. Ladle into bowls and garnish with thin avocado slices or a dollop of sour cream.

Soups and Salads

MOULTON BRAGS these days of having the second tallest water tower in Texas, but during the late 1930's this little central Texas town was the Garlic Capital of Texas. Garlic cultivation had just been introduced in Texas, and already the state's annual production ranked second only to California. The freshly picked garlic was stored beside the railroad tracks in what had been cotton warehouses and for several months each year the whole town reeked of garlic.

Blender Gazpacho

This is best served icy cold in a chilled glass mug on a hot summer day.

Serves 6

2 cups tomato juice, canned
1 cup fresh tomatoes, peeled and chopped
½ cup green pepper, chopped
½ cup celery, chopped
½ cup cucumber, chopped
¼ cup onion, chopped
2 tablespoons fresh parsley, minced
1 clove garlic, minced
2 tablespoons wine vinegar
2 tablespoons salad oil
1 teaspoon salt
½ teaspoon Worcestershire sauce
4 drops bottled hot pepper sauce
¼ teaspoon freshly ground pepper

Place all ingredients in blender container and blend for 30 seconds. Chill and serve.

PEANUTS TRAVELED over a large part of the world before taking root in Texas, one of the seven major peanut-producing states. Spanish explorers first found goobers in Peru and carried them back to Spain, where they were grown and from whence they were traded to Africa. Africans regarded the peanut as a plant possessed of a soul and they brought the nuts along when they came to the United States as slaves. Yankee soldiers went nuts for them during the Civil War, and peanuts were on their way to becoming a national snack. And Jimmy Carter didn't hurt their popularity.

Colonial Peanut Soup

A friend told us how good peanut soup was and suggested we try to find a recipe. This delicious soup recipe came from the Texas Peanut Producers Board.

Serves 6

2 tablespoons butter
2 tablespoons onion, chopped
1 stalk celery, thinly sliced
2 tablespoons flour
3 cups chicken broth
½ cup peanut butter
¼ teaspoon salt
2 teaspoons lemon juice
2 tablespoons roasted peanuts, chopped

Melt butter in saucepan over low heat; add onion and celery. Sauté until tender. Add flour and mix until well blended. Stir in chicken broth and simmer for 30 minutes. Remove from heat and strain broth. Stir peanut butter, salt and lemon juice into strained broth until smooth. Serve in mugs garnished with 1 teaspoon chopped peanuts.

Soups and Salads

THE SUPER AIRPORT of Dallas-Fort Worth is the second busiest airport in the United States, with more than 20 million passengers flying in and out each year. Just like any city, it has its own police department, fire department, post office and water and sewage system. With its restaurants, hotels, medical clinic, chapel and golf course, D-FW can take care of a person's every need—or fly you somewhere that can.

Cream of Tomato Soup with Rice

The fresh, rich taste of this soup makes it quite distinctive.

Serves 6

¼ cup onion, thinly sliced
6 tablespoons butter
1 carrot, diced very fine
3 cups canned tomatoes, sieved
1½ teaspoons salt
¼ teaspoon pepper
 Dash of soda
3 cups milk, hot
1 cup heavy cream, hot
1 cup cooked rice, hot

Saute' onion in butter for 1 minute. Add carrot and cook until tender. Add tomatoes which have been sieved to remove seeds and skins. Season and heat. Stir soda into tomato mixture and combine with hot milk and cream. Add hot rice, reheat and serve.

Soups and Salads

BON VIVANT that he was, William Sydney Porter (O. Henry) wrote often of food and drink in his short stories. Porter spent 15 years in Texas and, like so many others, cultivated a fondness for Mexican food. He was a regular patron of San Antonio's "Chili Queens," the street vendors of the 1890's, and the tamale stands of Austin inspired his infamous, hilarious poem, "Tamales."

Tortilla Soup

Serves 4

1 small onion, chopped
2 garlic cloves, mashed
1 4-ounce can green chiles, diced
2 tablespoons oil
1 8-ounce can stewed tomatoes
2 cups chicken broth
1 cup beef bouillon
1 teaspoon ground cumin
1 teaspoon chili powder
1 teaspoon salt
¼ teaspoon pepper
2 teaspoons Worchestershire sauce
1 cup Monterrey Jack or
   Cheddar cheese, grated
4 corn tortillas
   Oil for frying tortillas

Using a medium saucepan, sauté onion, garlic and green chiles in oil until soft. Add tomatoes, chicken broth and beef bouillon. Mix in spices and simmer for 1 hour.

Cut tortillas into quarters, then into ½-inch strips. Fry strips in hot oil until crisp and drain.

Add fried tortilla strips to soup and simmer 10 minutes. Ladle into bowls and top with shredded cheese.

Variation

If you are using ovenproof bowls for soup, place bowls under broiler for 4-5 minutes to melt cheese.

SAM BASS may have robbed banks and trains; but when he made a legimate purchase, he was one heck of a tipper: $20 for a sack of corn; $40 for biscuits, bacon, eggs and coffee; $4 for a gourdful of water. When Bass needed something, he generally needed it in a hurry; and he always paid in gold. He spent money as fast as he got it; and he was dead broke when he tried to rob his last bank, in Round Rock.

Portuguese Soup

The Inn at Brushy Creek in Round Rock serves this hearty soup with its marvelous blend of flavors. If you can't get to the Inn to enjoy Portuguese Soup as prepared by their chef, make and enjoy it at home.

Serves 8

1   cup onion, chopped
3   cloves garlic, chopped
3   tablespoons oil
½   pound garlic-flavored smoked pork sausage (Elgin type or Linguica)
5   cups beef stock
1   cup cooked kidney beans, undrained
½   head green cabbage, cored and chopped into medium pieces
6   small new potatoes, scrubbed and quartered
2-4 tablespoons vinegar
1   cup catsup
     Salt and pepper to taste

Using a 3-quart saucepan or kettle, sauté onion and garlic in oil until just transparent. Cut sausage into bite-sized pieces; add to vegetables and brown lightly. Add beef stock and remaining ingredients. Bring soup to a boil, stirring frequently. Reduce heat and simmer 35-45 minutes, stirring occasionally. Correct seasonings to taste.

The soup freezes well except for the potatoes, which disintegrate when soup is thawed and reheated. The flavor of the soup is best when refrigerated for a few days and reheated. It will keep for several days in the refrigerator.

Avocado and Tomato Salad

Serves 4

Shredded lettuce
2 avocados
1 tablespoon lime juice
2 medium tomatoes, skinned
4 slices bacon, cooked crisp

Buttermilk Dressing
½ cup buttermilk
4 tablespoons lemon juice
4 tablespoons oil
1 clove garlic, minced
2 tablespoons chives, minced
½ teaspoon salt

Prepare dressing several hours before serving by combining all ingredients in a pint jar. Chill. When ready to serve, make a bed of shredded lettuce on each of 4 salad plates. Peel avocados, cut in wedges and sprinkle with lime juice. Cut tomatoes in wedges and alternate with avocado wedges on lettuce. Drizzle dressing over tomato and avocado wedges and crumble bacon on top.

Kraut Salad

Serves 8-10

4 cups sauerkraut, drained
1 green pepper, chopped
½ red pepper, chopped, or
　 2 tablespoons pimento
1 large onion, diced
¾ cup celery, diced
½ cup grated carrots
¼ cup vinegar
½ cup salad oil
¾ cup sugar

Press excess juice from sauerkraut. Add green and red peppers (or use pimento for red color). Add onion, celery and carrots and mix gently. Combine vinegar, oil and sugar and pour over vegetables. Mix thoroughly and chill for several hours before serving.

Soups and Salads

SAN FELIPE DE AUSTIN had auspicious beginnings: first Anglo-American town in Texas (1823); first Anglo Capital of Texas; home to Stephen F. Austin, William B. Travis, Sam Houston, Jane Long. All settlers had to come here to get their land grants. Even the Texas Revolution had its beginnings at conventions held at San Felipe; but then its leaders moved to Washington-on-the-Brazos and never returned. San Felipe burned during the Runaway Scrape, was partially rebuilt and served as Austin County seat until an 1846 special election gave that honor to Bellville. Today San Felipe is not much larger than it was in its heyday, and Stephen F. Austin could probably still find his way home—an exact replica of the only home he owned in Texas stands in the state park which bears his name.

Broccoli and Cauliflower Salad

This crunchy salad appealed to everyone who tested it—even confirmed vegetable-haters.

Serves 8

1 pound fresh broccoli
1 small head cauliflower
2 large carrots, sliced
2 small zucchini, sliced
1 red onion, sliced and
  separated in rings

Wash and trim broccoli to make bite-sized flowerets. Wash cauliflower, remove stems, and separate into flowerets. Combine broccoli, cauliflower, carrots, zucchini and onion in a large bowl.

Dressing
⅔ cups mayonnaise
⅓ cup salad oil
½ cup salad vinegar
¼ cup sugar
1 teaspoon salt

Combine dressing ingredients and add to vegetables. Toss until thoroughly coated. Chill several hours before serving.

Soups and Salads

"THE EYES OF TEXAS," official song of the University of Texas at Austin, began as a student prank. University President William L. Prather had a habit of closing his speeches to students with the weighty admonition, "Remember, the eyes of Texas are upon you." John L. Sinclair took the phrase and twisted it into a song to the tune of "I've Been Working on the Railroad," for a 1903 student minstrel show.

'Eyes of Texas' Salad

Athens has a Black-Eyed Pea Jamboree every summer, and along with all the rest of the fun there is a Black-Eyed Pea Cookoff. Linda Martin won the cookoff in 1979 and 1980, and again in 1982 with this Grand Champion recipe.

Serves 8

1½ cups black-eyed peas, cooked and drained
1 cup rice, cooked
1 cup cooked chicken, finely chopped
¼ cup celery, chopped
¼ cup onion, chopped
¼ cup mayonnaise
½ teaspoon salt
1 teaspoon pepper
Dash hot sauce

Combine cooled black-eyed peas, rice and chicken. Add remaining ingredients, blend well and pack into an oiled 5½-cup mold. Refrigerate until set. Unmold and spread with Avocado Topping.

Avocado Topping
1 avocado, mashed
½ cup sour cream
1 teaspoon garlic salt
½ cup mayonnaise
½ teaspoon Worcestershire sauce
¼ teaspoon salt
½ teaspoon lemon juice

Blend ingredients together until smooth. Spread over black-eyed pea ring as though frosting a cake.

Soups and Salads

CONVICTS WITH HEAVY iron balls chained to their ankles labored mightily to quarry the limestone used in building the State Capitol. The year was 1885 and the place was a hill now known as Convict Hill in Oak Hill, on the outskirts of Austin. The Capitol Building Commission decided that all stone used in the Capitol should be native to Texas; so limestone from Convict Hill was used for the interior and dome walls, and pink granite from Granite Mountain near Marble Falls was used for the exterior. Convict labor was an economy measure. The Building Contractor for the State Capitol received his pay in the form of a big chunk of the Texas Panhandle.

Convict Hill Restaurant Cucumber Salad

Convict Hill Restaurant in Oak Hill features Texas atmosphere, good food and one of the finest wine lists in all Texas. This salad is one of its specialties.

Serves 6-8

3 medium cucumbers, scored and thinly sliced
1 medium yellow onion, cut in thin strips
2 medium tomatoes, each cut in 6 wedges
1 tablespoon cornstarch
2 tablespoons water
1 cup tarragon vinegar
1 cup sugar
1 cup sunflower oil
2 tablespoons salt
1 tablespoon black pepper
2 teaspoons white pepper
½ cup freeze-dried chives

Place cucumbers, onion and tomatoes in medium salad bowl. Mix cornstarch and water in a small saucepan. Add vinegar and bring to a simmer over low heat, stirring constantly. Simmer until mixture becomes clear and slightly thickened. Add remaining ingredients and cool. Pour over vegetables and toss. Refrigerate 20-30 minutes before serving. Any remaining marinade may be refrigerated 2-3 weeks.

Soups and Salads

STAGECOACH LINES carried mail and passengers across Texas over barely passable roads through areas where ambush by Indians or outlaws was a constant possibility. Lines like the Butterfield Overland Mail traveled day and night, stopping every few miles for fresh horses and a meal of cold beans, cornbread and coffee. Stagecoaches traveled Texas for only twenty years, but live on in imagination and Hollywood westerns.

Cole Slaw With Horseradish Dressing

Serves 4

3   cups finely shredded cabbage
1   large apple, sliced
¾   cup dairy sour cream
2   tablespoons prepared horseradish
    Salt and pepper to taste

Mix cabbage and apple together in a medium bowl. Mix sour cream, horseradish, salt and pepper until blended. Pour over cabbage and apple mixture and mix gently. Chill at least 1 hour before serving.

Southern Cabbage Slaw

Serves 6

4   cups cabbage, finely shredded
1   large onion, finely chopped
2   carrots, shredded
1   green pepper, finely chopped
½   cup white vinegar
½   cup sugar
½   cup oil
1   teaspoon salt
½   teaspoon celery seed
1   teaspoon dry mustard

Combine cabbage, onion, carrots, and green pepper in a large bowl. Place remaining ingredients in a small saucepan and bring to a boil. Lower heat and simmer about 2 minutes. Pour over cabbage mixture. Cool and refrigerate overnight. This keeps several days in the refrigerator.

YOU COULD CALL HIM Johnny-on-the-Spot: despite his deafness, Erastus "Deaf" Smith was an ace scout and quickly rose to prominence in the Texian army. As scout, he set up the Battle of Concepcion and the Grass Fight, and he brought the Widow Dickenson and her baby back from the fallen Alamo. When Sam Houston wanted Vince's Bridge destroyed, so that neither his Texians nor Santa Anna's troops could escape the field of San Jacinto, he called on Deaf Smith. Smith briefly captained a company of Rangers after the War, and died in November of 1837, when the Republic was barely a year old.

Deaf Smith County Corn Salad

Serves 8-10

¾   cup vinegar
¾   cup corn oil
¾   cup sugar
1   teaspoon salt
½   teaspoon pepper
1   cup green pepper, chopped
1   cup celery, chopped
½   cup green onions and tops, chopped
1   16-ounce can shoepeg corn
1   8-ounce can small peas
1   2-ounce jar pimentos, diced

Combine vinegar, oil, sugar, salt and pepper in saucepan and bring to a boil. Set aside to cool. Place green pepper, celery and onions in large bowl. Drain corn, peas and pimentos and combine with vegetables. Pour vinegar and oil mixture over the vegetables and mix: refrigerate for several hours.

This salad stays crisp and fresh for several days if refrigerated.

M.H. CROCKETT of Manor was the father of the Texas spinach industry. He began shipping small batches of locally-grown spinach to the northern markets in 1907, while still a University of Texas student. "It can't be done on a large scale," the experts told him. Crockett ignored them, and Austin became the center of the Texas spinach industry—indeed, the country's second largest spinach shipping point. By 1922, Crockett was considered a national authority on spinach, and by 1928 he was one of the country's largest producers.

Fresh Spinach and Mushroom Salad

Serves 6-8

1   **pound fresh spinach, carefully washed**
½   **pound fresh mushrooms, sliced**
½   **medium red onion, sliced**
2   **tablespoons sesame seeds, toasted**
6   **slices bacon, cooked crisp**

Dressing
1   **cup salad oil**
4   **tablespoons sour cream**
5   **tablespoons wine vinegar**
½   **teaspoon salt**
½   **teaspoon dry mustard**
2   **tablespoons sugar**
    Black pepper to taste
2   **teaspoons parsley, minced**
2   **garlic cloves, mashed**

Remove stems and heavy veins from spinach. Combine with mushrooms and onion slices in a large salad bowl. Pour half dressing over the salad and toss. Add more dressing as needed to thoroughly coat spinach without drowning it. Add sesame seeds and toss again. Top with bacon and serve.

Blend oil into sour cream. Gradually mix in vinegar. Combine with remaining ingredients in a pint jar. Shake well and refrigerate several hours.

THE UNIVERSITY OF TEXAS was created in 1839, but classes did not begin until 1883. It's a wonder the University ever got off the ground; a contemporary enemy declared universities to be "hotbeds of immorality, prolifigacy, and licentiousness." Once started, UT limped along on a minimal budget until 1923, when oil was discovered beneath a portion of the University's two million acres of West Texas. Thanks to that oil, UT's permanent endowment fund is the second largest in the country.

Spinach and Pea Salad

This recipe is from Loraine Jackson, Staff Coordinator of Cook 'em Horns, *a cookbook published by The Ex-Student's Association of the University of Texas in celebration of the University's Centennial. This great cookbook is now in its third edition.*

Serves 4

10 ounces fresh spinach	**Dressing**
1 10-ounce package frozen garden peas, thawed	½ cup catsup
	1 cup salad oil
1 5-ounce can water chestnuts, sliced	½ cup sugar
	⅓ cup cider vinegar
7 strips bacon, cooked crisp	1 tablespoon Worcestershire sauce
1 hard boiled egg, sliced	1 onion, grated
	1 teaspoon salt (optional)

Wash spinach carefully, remove stems and large veins, and cut into strips. Place spinach in large salad bowl, add peas (uncooked) and water chestnuts. Crumble bacon in large pieces and add. Chill until ready to add Dressing. Combine Dressing ingredients and blend well. Pour enough Dressing on salad to coat thoroughly. Toss gently and garnish with slices of egg.

SOME THINGS are a long time in coming. With its burgeoning high tech industry, Austin is now touted as the up-and-coming capital of the Silicon Universe. But such grandiose dreams are nothing new: Austin was named the capital of Texas in 1839, back when this was the edge of the western frontier. After killing a buffalo where the capitol now stands, then-President of the Republic Mirabeau B. Lamar looked down towards the Colorado River and declared, "This should be the seat of a future empire." Nearly 150 years later, Lamar's dream may be coming true.

Molded Garden Salad

Serves 10

2 large packages lemon gelatin
3 cups hot water
3 tablespoons vinegar
½ teaspoon salt
1 cup mayonnaise
2 tablespoons onion, grated
¾ cup cauliflower, diced
¾ cup carrots, shredded
¾ cup celery, diced
¾ cup radishes, sliced

Dissolve gelatin in hot water. Add vinegar, salt and mayonnaise. Stir until mixed. Chill until gelatin is thick but not set. Beat with an electric mixer at low speed until fluffy. Fold in vegetables and turn into a 2-quart dish or mold. Chill and serve.

Macaroni Salad

This hearty salad should be made several hours before serving to give flavors time to blend. It's a great take-along for picnics or tail-gating at football games.

Serves 12

1 12-ounce package elbow macaroni	1½ teaspoons salt
1 cucumber, seeded and chopped	1 teaspoon sugar
1 bunch green onions, sliced	½ teaspoon white pepper
1 cup celery, sliced	½ teaspoon celery salt
1 cup (4-ounces) Cheddar cheese, cubed or cut in strips	¼ cup pickle relish
	1 cup cherry tomatoes, halved Parsley for garnish

Dressing
3 cups mayonnaise
¾ cups sour cream
1 cup light cream
3 tablespoons Durkee's sauce
2 teaspoons Dijon mustard

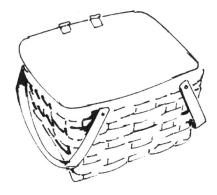

Cook macaroni according to package directions. Drain, cool and add remaining ingredients, except for tomatoes. Mix dressing ingredients together. Toss macaroni mixture with dressing and refrigerate 6-8 hours. Add cherry tomatoes just before serving; toss and garnish with sprigs of parsley.

BACK IN THE EARLY DAYS of Texas, a good bee hunter was worth his weight in—well, honey. Many frontier Texians ate venison and bear steak day in and day out, and honey was often the only food to relieve this monotony. Bee hunters knew that once a bee gathered a load of nectar it flew in a beeline to its hive. When a hunter found a bee, he'd follow it home and chop an X into the tree containing its hive as a sign of pre-emption.

Honey Dressing

Yields 1½ cups

1 teaspoon dry mustard
1 teaspoon paprika
1 teaspoon celery seed
¼ teaspoon salt
½ cup honey
2 tablespoons lemon juice
2 tablespoons vinegar
½ cup salad oil

Mix dry ingredients. Add honey, lemon juice and vinegar and mix with a whisk or rotary beater. Add oil slowly while mixing. Serve over citrus or fresh fruit salad or use for Honeyed Bananas.

Honeyed Bananas

Serves 6

6 bananas　　　　½ cup Honey Dressing

Place Honey Dressing in medium saucepan. Bring to a simmer over low heat. Peel bananas, add to honey dressing; cook over low heat, turning gently, 2 or 3 minutes or until bananas are hot and glazed.

Soups and Salads

STEPHEN F. AUSTIN, "The Father of Texas," was at first an unwilling patriarch. Colonizing Spanish Texas was his father's idea. Stephen reluctantly agreed to partner in the scheme; but when Moses Austin died a few months later, Stephen was left to carry on under trying conditions. Austin originally opposed the Texas Revolution because he did not think the time was ripe for Texas independence. Elected commander-in-chief of the revolutionary army in 1835, he soon stepped down to go to New Orleans to seek U.S. aid. Defeated in Texas' first presidential election by Sam Houston, Austin died of pneumonia December 27, 1836, at his Brazoria County plantation — land-rich but money-poor, unmarried and 43 years old.

Mary's Fruit Salad

Serves 4

4   bananas
2   tablespoons frozen orange juice concentrate
3   red delicious apples, diced
¼   cup unsalted peanuts
½   cup raisins
4   tablespoons yogurt (optional)

Slice bananas into a medium bowl and add orange juice concentrate. Stir to coat bananas. Add apples, peanuts and raisins and mix. Chill for 1 hour. Serve on lettuce leaves, and top with yogurt if desired.

Texas Fruit Tray

A big, beautiful arrangement of fruit can become the edible centerpiece of a brunch or buffet table. Why not serve one that uses only fruits grown in Texas?

Serves 16

1	Pecos cantaloupe
¼	Luling watermelon
4	Mission oranges
2	Ruby Red grapefruit from the Rio Grande Valley
1	pint Poteet strawberries
1	pint East Texas blueberries
1	cup wild dewberries
	Mint leaves for garnish

Remove rind from cantaloupe and watermelon. Seed cantaloupe and cut into 16 crescents. Cut watermelon into 3-inch wedges and remove visible seeds. Peel oranges and cut into ½-inch cartwheels. Peel and section grapefruit. Wash strawberries, blueberries and dewberries. Arrange attractively on a large tray and garnish with mint leaves. Serve with Poppyseed Dressing.

Poppy Seed Dressing

Yields 1½ cups

2	tablespoons onion, minced
⅓	cup sugar
1	teaspoon dry mustard
1	teaspoon salt
⅓	cup vinegar
1	cup vegetable oil
1	tablespoon poppyseed

Combine all ingredients except poppyseed in blender container. Blend at slowest speed for 30 seconds. Pour into a pint jar, add poppyseed and refrigerate until ready to serve. This will keep 2 weeks if refrigerated.

Soups and Salads

WHEN TEXAS BECAME A STATE, thousands of pioneers poured in from other states and countries. Among this wave of new Texans were people named Matsler, Smelser, and Gillett, my great-grandparents. A special part of our family reunions is the retelling of stories of how our ancestors came to Texas and of the hardships and adventures experienced as they made new homes in central and west Texas. They, and thousands like them, had faith, courage and determination beyond our comprehension.

Matsler's Fruit Delight

This unusual salad was served at a recent family reunion along with dozens of examples of the best of Texas cooking. The book was almost finished, but the recipe was so different and so good it had to be included.

Serves 6

1 8-ounce carton small curd cottage cheese
1 3-ounce package orange gelatin
1 8-ounce container frozen whipped topping, thawed
1 8-ounce can crushed pineapple, drained
1 8-ounce can Mandarin oranges, drained

Combine cottage cheese and dry orange gelatin. Add whipped topping and mix well. Fold in the pineapple and mandarin oranges until thoroughly blended. Chill and serve.

Soups and Salads

A LARGE ROUND ROCK in the middle of Brushy Creek was a marker for the Tonkawa and Comanche Indians who battled fiercely for control of the area with its good water, abundant hunting and gently rolling prairies. Early settlers found the cool, clear water and shady trees near the rock a wonderful place to camp and rest on their trek westward. Eventually the town of Round Rock grew nearby, and the people who live there today enjoy the fine quality of life still offered by their surroundings.

Round Rock Frozen Salad

Kids love this melt-in-your-mouth salad!

Serves 10-12

2 3-ounce packages lemon gelatin
2 cups boiling water
2 3-ounce packages cream cheese, softened
2 cups whipped topping
1 15¼-ounce can crushed pineapple, with juice
1 banana, diced
1 cup mini-marshmallows
1 cup fresh or frozen strawberries, sliced

Dissolve gelatin in boiling water. Mix cream cheese with 2 tablespoons of whipped topping. Gradually blend gelatin into cream cheese mixture. Add pineapple, banana and marshmallows. Fold in rest of whipped topping and add strawberries. Pour into a 13x9-inch pan and freeze.

Remove salad from freezer 10 minutes before serving.

MAIN DISHES

From Texas...
with love

Main Dishes

THE BADU HOUSE of Llano is an historic building that has been restored and made into a charming inn with guest rooms and wonderful food. Ann Ruff, whose vision, hard work and culinary skill has made the Badu House so special, is also author of several books about Texas and contributor of this elegant and easy recipe, a Badu House favorite.

Ann's Badu House Chicken

Serves 6

12 chicken breasts, skinned and boned
24 slices canned jalapeno peppers, seeded
12 slices bacon, uncooked
1 medium bottle Italian dressing
1 large jar pimentos, chopped

Fold each chicken breast around 2 slices jalapeno peppers. (If you like a hotter chicken, use 3 slices.) Wrap a slice of bacon around the chicken breast and place in a large cooking bag that has been lightly dusted with flour. Pour Italian dressing over the breasts and sprinkle with pimentos. Marinate in refrigerator overnight. When ready to cook, puncture bag, place in a large baking dish and bake at 350° for 1 hour.

This is delicious served with rice. Allow 2 chicken breasts per person; but if there are any left, they may be frozen in marinade and reheated with no loss of flavor.

Chicken and Asparagus Casserole

Serves 10

4 tablespoons flour
4 tablespoons butter
2½ cups chicken broth
1½ cups American cheese, grated
5 cups chicken, cooked and cubed
1 cup canned artichoke hearts
1 10-ounce package frozen asparagus, thawed

Blend flour and butter in a medium saucepan. Stir over medium heat until bubbly. Gradually add chicken broth, stirring constantly. Add 1 cup cheese; stir until melted. Place half of chicken in a buttered 3-quart casserole and cover with 1 cup of cheese sauce. Layer artichoke hearts, asparagus, remaining chicken and remaining cheese sauce. Sprinkle remaining grated cheese over top and bake at 375° for 30 minutes.

Forty-Clove Chicken

This tasty recipe was contributed by Jo Ann Horton, Editor of the Goat Gap Gazette, known as the "Bible of the Chili World." She is also the Dining Out Editor for "Houston Monthly Magazine"; and she loves garlic, used generously in this dish.

Serves 4-6

1 frying chicken, cut up
40 garlic cloves, peeled
4 stalks celery, cut in 1-inch pieces
1 lemon
¼ cup olive oil
½ cup dry white wine
¼ cup dry vermouth
1 teaspoon oregano
2 teaspoons basil
6 springs parsley, minced
Pinch of crushed red pepper
Salt and pepper to taste

Place chicken pieces in shallow baking pan, skin side up. Spread garlic and celery over chicken. Squeeze juice from lemon, pour over chicken. Cut lemon rind in pieces and scatter on top. Combine remaining ingredients and pour over chicken. Cover with foil and bake at 375° for 40 minutes. Uncover and bake an additional 15 minutes.

Main Dishes

JANUARY 1837 is usually given as the beginning of the city of Houston, Texas' largest city (its million-and-a-half residents make it the nation's fifth most populous). It was then that the Allen Brothers made their first multiple sales of lots. However, the brothers had bought 6,642 acres on Buffalo Bayou five months earlier—for $9,428; and in September and October of 1836, surveyor Gail Borden (he of condensed milk fame) laid out the streets of Houston. Borden was ridiculed for his prophecy that great "vehicles would cruise through the streets of Houston...". He made the main east-west street 100 feet wide and named it Texas Avenue; and laid out the other streets 80 feet wide.

Galleria Chicken Cutlets

These tender chicken cutlets may be prepared ahead, except for the final few minutes of baking, for an attractive and delicious main course when entertaining.

Serves 4

4 chicken breasts,
  boned and skinned
1½ cups dry bread or cracker
  crumbs, finely crushed
½ cup grated Parmesan
  or Romano cheese
2 tablespoons parsley flakes
½ teaspoon garlic salt
2 eggs, beaten
1 tablespoon water
4 tablespoons corn oil
1 cup sliced mushrooms
½ cup butter, melted
  Thin lemon slices and
  parsley for garnish

Divide each chicken breast into 2 cutlets. Combine bread or cracker crumbs, cheese, parsley flakes and garlic salt. Mix beaten eggs and water together. Dip each cutlet into egg mixture, then into crumb mixture. Heat oil in large skillet and brown cutlets on each side until golden brown. Remove cutlets to flat baking dish.

Sauté mushrooms briefly in oil used to brown cutlets. Spoon mushrooms over cutlets. In small saucepan, melt butter and lemon juice. Pour over chicken and mushrooms. Bake in 350° oven for 20-25 minutes (allow 30-35 minutes if prepared ahead and cooled). Garnish with thin lemon slices and sprigs of parsley.

Main Dishes

THE KING RANCH may be the most famous spread in America, and this just might be the best-loved recipe in Texas. It was sent in, with only slight variations, by good cooks all over the state. How the dish earned its name, its only connection to the illustrious ranch, nobody knows.

King Ranch Chicken Casserole

Serves 8

1   10¾-ounce can cream of chicken soup
1   10¾-ounce can cream of mushroom soup
2   cups chicken broth
1   10-ounce can Ro-Tel Tomatoes and Green Chiles
12 tortillas, cut in pieces
1   3-4 pound chicken, cooked and cut into bite-sized pieces
1   large onion, chopped
2   cups grated American cheese

Combine soups, chicken broth and tomatoes and set aside. Oil a 3-quart casserole. Layer half of tortilla pieces, half of chicken, half of onion and half of cheese in the casserole. Pour half of chicken broth mixture over layers. Repeat layers of tortillas, chicken and onion, then pour remaining chicken broth over top with remaining cheese. Bake at 350° for 45-60 minutes. This may be frozen and reheated and will still taste great.

Lakeway Chicken Salad

Artichokes, rice and chicken combine to make a great luncheon salad which never fails to bring enthusiastic compliments.

Serves 8

1 package chicken-flavored Rice-A-Roni
6 green onions, sliced
½ cup green pepper, minced
¼ cup stuffed green olives, sliced
⅓ cup mayonnaise
2 6-ounce jars artichoke hearts, drained (reserve marinade)
¼ teaspoon curry powder
2½ cups cooked chicken, cut into bite-sized pieces
Parsley

Prepare Rice-A-Roni according to directions on package, omitting butter. Drain and combine with onions, green pepper and olives. Mix mayonnaise, marinade from artichokes and curry powder. Add to rice mixture; stir just enough to mix. Add chicken and artichoke hearts and toss lightly. Chill and serve, garnished with parsley.

Turkey Tetrazinni

You could use this recipe for leftover turkey, but it is good enough to merit cooking a turkey just to make it. Or you may substitute chicken for the turkey and have Chicken Tetrazinni.

Serves 16-18

1 10-12 pound turkey, cooked and cut in bite-sized pieces
1 7-ounce package noodles, cooked
2 tablespoons butter
1 green pepper, diced
1 stalk celery, diced
2 medium onions, grated
½ pound butter, melted
1 cup flour
4 cups milk
½ pound American cheese, grated
½ pound sharp cheese, grated
1 can cream of mushroom soup
  Garlic salt, Lawry's Seasoned Salt, and paprika to taste

Topping
½ cup butter, melted
1 small box Ritz crackers, finely crushed

Combine turkey with noodles and set aside. Melt butter in large skillet and sauté green pepper, celery and onion. Remove vegetables and combine with turkey and noodles. Melt butter in skillet; add flour and stir until smooth. Add milk gradually, stirring constantly until sauce thickens. Add cheeses and soup. Combine cheese sauce with turkey mixture and add seasonings to taste. Pour into a 6-quart casserole or two 3-quart baking dishes. For Topping, mix butter and cracker crumbs and sprinkle over tetrazinni. Bake at 350° for 35-40 minutes or until bubbly.

YOU KNOW TIMES ARE HARD when even the grog shops shut down—that's exactly how poor the Republic of Texas was during most of its ten-year existence. Even the great Sam Houston passed the summer of 1840 without a red cent in his pocket. Which is not to say there was no commerce—just no hard money. Folks bartered: "Cotton for sugar and coffee, Bacon for boots, Corn for Calomel and quinine and whiskey, beef for brandy" reads the account book of one early Texas trader. Beef on the hoof was the closest thing to a standard currency—a cow and calf were valued at ten dollars most anywhere in the Republic.

Brazos River Stew

Hungry family and friends will enjoy this hearty stew.

Serves 6

3 slices bacon
1 pound stew meat
1 16-ounce can tomatoes
2 cups beef broth or bouillon
1 cup water
2 ribs celery, sliced
2 medium onions, chopped
2 garlic cloves, minced
1 ounce Worcestershire sauce
1 teaspoon chili powder
1 tablespoon flour
   Salt and pepper to taste
4 medium carrots, sliced thick
4 small potatoes
1 8-ounce can corn

Fry bacon in a Dutch oven or large stew pot. Remove bacon and drain on paper towel. Add stew meat to pan and sear. Lower heat and add tomatoes, beef broth or bouillon, water, celery, onion, garlic, Worcestershire sauce and chili powder. Cover and simmer 2 hours. Remove ¼ cup broth from stew, cool, and mix with flour. Add flour mixture to stew. Salt and pepper as needed. Add carrots and potatoes and cook 30 minutes. Add corn and bacon; cook another 5 minutes. Serve in large bowls.

Main Dishes

From Bob Moore:

Circuit Rider Chili

Bob Moore's recipe took first place at Frank X. Tolbert's 14th Annual World Championship Chili Cook-Off at Terlingua, Texas in 1980. Tolbert's Cook-Off at Terlingua is the granddaddy, the original, of Texas' chili-cooking contests.

Serves 10 hearty appetites

5 pounds boneless sirloin tip roast (remove all visible fat and connecting tissue) cut into 3/8-inch cubes

4 tablespoons kidney fat, minced

2 medium white onions, minced

1 12-ounce bottle or can beer (not light)

1 8-ounce can tomato sauce

1 8-ounce can hot water

12 ounces beef stock

6 large garlic cloves mashed in 1 tablespoon oil until puree is formed

5 tablespoons paprika (Mexican)

2 teaspoons salt

1 tablespoon enhancer

1½ teaspoons pepper

11 tablespoons unblended chili powder (he grinds his own with various Mexican chiles)

5½ tablespoons cumin (fine grind, Mexican)

1 teaspoon oregano

¼ teaspoon ground chile japones or chile arbol (for additional heat)

If you don't want to make your own chili powder, Bob suggests you use 10 tablespoons of a good commercial chili powder, cut the cumin to 2½ tablespoons, cut the paprika to 2 tablespoons and omit the oregano.

In a frying pan, brown meat with rendered kidney fat until gray in color. (He browns about 2 pounds of meat at a time with 1 tablespoon rendered kidney fat.) Return meat and natural juices to cooking pot. Sauté onions in 1 tablespoon rendered kidney fat until translucent. Return to pot.

Add beer, tomato sauce, hot water, beef stock, ½ of the mashed garlic mixture, 2 tablespoons paprika, 1 teaspoon salt, flavor enhancer, 1 teaspoon pepper. Simmer over low heat 2 hours until meat is tender. Be sure pot has a tight lid, as this will help the tenderizing process. Stir occasionally.

When meat is tender, add remaining garlic mixture, unblended chili powder, cumin, 3 tablespoons paprika, oregano, 1 teaspoon salt, ½ teaspoon pepper and chili japones. Continue cooking 15 more minutes. Turn heat off and let set 1-2 hours so that the flavor of the spices is absorbed, then turn heat back on and continue to simmer for 1 additional hour. Total cooking time is 3 hours, 15 minutes.

Chimichangas

Chimichangas are usually fried, but these are baked and are crisp and tasty.

Serves 4

Filling
- ½ teaspoon salt
- 1 pound lean ground beef
- 1 clove garlic, crushed
- 1 teaspoon ground cumin
- 1 teaspoon dried oregano
- ¼ cup canned chopped chiles
- ¼ cup bottled taco sauce
- ¼ cup sour cream
- 2 tablespoons cider vinegar

Sprinkle salt in a medium skillet and place over medium heat. Add beef, garlic and spices. Cook and stir with a fork until meat crumbles and loses its pink color. Stir in remaining filling ingredients, remove from heat and cool.

Assembly
- ½ cup butter or margarine
- 6 large flour tortillas
- 4 ounces Cheddar cheese, shredded
- ½ cup sour cream
- ½ cup bottled picante sauce
- 2 avocados, sliced; or guacamole

Melt butter or margarine in a 10-inch skillet. Place each tortilla in warm butter until soft; drain and place on a flat surface. Mound a large spoonful of filling in center of tortilla and fold envelope fashion to seal filling inside. Place tortillas seam side down in a large baking dish.

Bake in a 450° oven for 15 minutes. Sprinkle with cheese and return to oven for a few seconds to melt cheese. Watch carefully as they burn easily. Serve with sour cream, picante sauce and avocados or guacamole.

Colonel's Favorite Barbecued Beef Brisket

This brisket can be cut with a fork and is good with or without the barbecue sauce.

Serves 10-12

7 pounds beef brisket, trimmed
2 teaspoons onion salt
1 tablespoon celery salt
1 teaspoon garlic salt
4 teaspoons monosodium glutamate
2 tablespoons Worcestershire sauce
1½ tablespoons liquid smoke

Rub brisket with onion, celery, garlic salt and monosodium glutamate, and let stand for about 30 minutes. Place in a roaster and pour Worchestershire sauce and liquid smoke over surface of roast. Cover and refrigerate several hours.

Drain off marinade, wrap brisket, fatty side up, in heavy duty aluminum foil and seal. Bake 5 hours at 300°. Allow to cool. Slice thinly across the grain, place in a baking dish, cover with Texas Barbecue Sauce and bake 20 minutes at 325°.

Texas Barbecue Sauce

This sauce is good for anything you want to barbecue, but any barbecue sauce that contains sugar will carmelize if cooked more than a few minutes, particularly if used when grilling.

Yields 1 quart

½ cup butter
¼ cup vinegar
¼ cup Worcestershire sauce
¼ cup sugar
   (more if sweet sauce preferred)
   Salt, pepper and garlic salt to taste

2 cups catsup
¼ cup lemon juice
½ cup water
1 large onion, chopped
2 teaspoons Tabasco

Combine ingredients and simmer 20 minutes over medium heat.

Enchilada-Taco Torte

Serve these by lining up the ingredients in order: a plate of warm tortillas; a chafing dish of hot meat sauce; bowls of shredded lettuce, chopped onions and tomatoes; another chafing dish of cheese sauce; and bowls of sliced avocados and ripe olives. Let your family and friends assemble their own creations.

Serves 4

Meat Sauce
- 1 tablespoon oil
- 1 pound ground beef
- 1 10-ounce can enchilada sauce

Cheese Sauce
- 2 tablespoons butter
- ½ medium onion, chopped
- 1 10-ounce can Ro-Tel Tomatoes and Green Chiles
- 1 pound processed cheese, cubed

Presentation
- ½ cup oil
- 8 corn tortillas
- ½ head lettuce, shredded
- 1 large onion, chopped
- 2 large ripe tomatoes, skinned and chopped
- 2 ripe avocados, sliced
- ½ cup ripe olives, sliced

Heat oil in a skillet; add ground beef and stir until crumbled and lightly browned. Add enchilada sauce and mix.

To make cheese sauce, heat butter in a saucepan; add onion and sauté until soft. Mash tomatoes and add with cheese cubes. Heat until cheese is melted.

When ready to serve, pour oil in a medium skillet and heat. Dip tortillas in oil long enough to soften, drain and cover to keep warm. To assemble, place a tortilla on a plate, cover with hot meat sauce and top with another tortilla. Spread lettuce, onions and tomatoes on tortilla and ladle cheese sauce over top of vegetables. Surround torte with avocado slices and sprinkle with olives.

Main Dishes

THESE DAYS a lot of us take Houston's Astrodome almost for granted. Yet it was the *first* fully air-conditioned enclosed domed multi-purpose sports stadium in the world. And without the Astrodome, the world wouldn't have Astroturf. The natural grass first planted needed sunlight, but sunlight through glass is blinding to anyone chasing a fly ball. And let's not forget the Dome's five restaurants either. The Astrodome is the biggest single beer account in Texas.

Houston Meat and Cheese Pie

Serves 4-6

½ pound ground beef
½ cup mayonnaise
½ cup milk
2 eggs
2 tablespoons flour
¾ cup Cheddar cheese, grated
¾ cup Swiss cheese, grated
⅓ cup sliced green onions
   Salt and pepper to taste
1 9-inch unbaked pie shell

Brown meat in a medium skillet and set aside. Blend mayonnaise, milk, eggs and flour until smooth. Stir in meat, cheese, onion, salt and pepper. Turn mixture into unbaked pastry shell. Bake at 350° for 35-40 minutes. This freezes well if you have any left over.

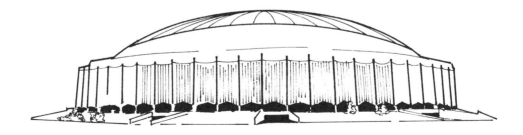

CHILI COOK-OFFS provide a favorite excuse for Texans to travel hundreds of miles to demonstrate their ability to make the best, or the most unusual, bowl of chili to be found anywhere. What makes good chili is a matter of personal opinion, and passionate arguments develop as opinions are exchanged. Basically, chili is any kind of meat chopped and cooked for a long time with chile peppers and spices. It's where you go from there that makes all the difference.

L. T. Felty's Chili

L. T. Felty of Waxahachie is a well-known chilihead and "official expert chili cook advisor to the governor." He judges and participates in more than 50 chili cook-offs a year, and is renowned for his showmanship as well as for his good chili.

Serves 15

5	pounds lean beef, coarsely ground
1	pound suet
1	medium onion
2	garlic pods, pressed
1	ounce ground cumin seed
1½	ounces Gebhardt's Chili Powder
1	pint water or tomato juice
1	tablespoon salt
	Black or red pepper to taste

Place suet in bottom of a large, heavy pot and heat until suet is "melted out." Add meat to suet and heat, stirring occasionally, until meat changes from pink to gray. (This should take about 30 minutes.) Add onion, garlic, cumin, chili powder and water. Cook until meat is tender, 1½-2 hours. Add salt and black or red pepper, then eat and enjoy.

A TEXAN'S PRIDE in being a Texan is hard for non-Texans to understand. Texas fought its own War of Independence and was a republic long enough to foster a strong sense of nationalism. The single star in the Texas flag symbolizes Texas' solitary stand in its fight for independence and gives the state the name "The Lone Star State."

Lone Star Chicken-Fried Steak

No Texas cookbook can claim authenticity without including a chicken-fried steak recipe. There are many variations, but all are breaded, tenderized steak, fried and served with cream gravy.

Serves 5

1½ pounds round steak, tenderized
1 cup flour
1 teaspoon salt
Pepper
2 eggs, slightly beaten
½ cup milk
Oil for frying

Gravy
6 tablespoons bacon or pan drippings
6 tablespoons flour
3 cups hot milk
Salt and pepper

Trim steak and cut into 5 pieces. Combine flour, salt and pepper. Dredge all steak pieces in flour mixture until lightly coated. Combine eggs and milk. Dip steak into egg mixture and dredge again in flour. Heat ½ inch of oil in a heavy skillet. Place steaks in skillet and fry until golden brown on both sides.

To make gravy, remove steaks to warm oven, retaining 6 tablespoons of drippings (or use bacon drippings). Add flour. Cook and stir until flour begins to brown. Add hot milk and stir until thickened. Season with salt and pepper to taste and pour over warm steaks. Or, if you prefer, serve gravy on the side.

MORE THAN any other symbol perhaps, the Longhorn represents Texas. After the Civil War Longhorns outnumbered people in Texas 9 to 1. Five million Texas Longhorns were driven north to market in 15 years, creating the range cattle industry in the process. When other breeds of cattle proved more profitable, the rangy native fell into disfavor with cattlemen; and the Texas Longhorn nearly became extinct. Today, humans outnumber Longhorns in Texas by nearly 500 to 1; and scientists are discovering the Longhorns are a genetic goldmine for an ailing cattle industry.

Longhorn Short Ribs

Serves 6

4 pounds beef short ribs
1½ cups beef broth
1 onion, sliced
⅓ cup flour
3 tablespoons butter, softened
1 garlic clove, finely chopped
   Salt and pepper to taste
½ cup beer

Place short ribs in a small roasting pan and brown in a 500° oven for 15 minutes. Pour off fat, add beef broth and onion, cover and lower heat to 350°. Cook 2 hours.

To make gravy, brown flour in a medium skillet over low heat. Remove from heat, mix in butter to form a paste and gradually add beef broth from pan, stirring with each addition. Return to heat and cook until gravy thickens. Add garlic and salt and pepper to taste. Add beer; stir, and pour over ribs. Heat 15 minutes. Serve on a platter surrounded with broiled tomato halves, tiny carrots and parsley potatoes.

Main Dishes

MESQUITE WOOD may be the current darling of the barbecue set, but the thorny tree is good for more than just briskets and punctured tires. Cattle and South Texas kids like mesquite beans raw. Indians processed the bean pods into soup, bread and beer. Desperate Anglo pioneers sometimes made "coffee" from dried and roasted mesquite beans. A sticky gum exuded from the tree was used for mending cracked pottery and as a hair preparation good for dying the hair black.

Mesquite-Smoked Fajitas

Fajitas are very near the top of the list of Texans' favorite foods. They don't have to be smoked over mesquite wood, but it does add a distinctive flavor. The skirt steak is not tender, so it is important to marinate it overnight.

Serves 4

2 pounds skirt steak
Lemon pepper
1 12-ounce can of beer
1 8-ounce bottle Italian dressing
8 flour tortillas
Sour cream
Grated cheese
Picante sauce or Pico de Gallo sauce

Trim skirt steak to remove membrane and bits of fat. Rub meat with lemon pepper and place in a refrigerator dish. Combine beer and Italian dressing and pour over meat. Marinate overnight. Grill over hot charcoal about 8 minutes to a side, basting with marinade.

Remove meat to cutting board and slice thinly across grain. Steam tortillas until soft. Place spoonful of steak slices on each tortilla, top with picante or Pico de Gallo sauce, shredded lettuce, grated cheese and sour cream, and roll.

Main Dishes

IN THE DAYS BEFORE REFRIGERATION, Texas communities often organized beef clubs to ensure a daily supply of fresh meat on the table during summer— generally from the first Saturday before Easter to the first norther in the fall. Each family donated one calf, and each Saturday morning a calf was slaughtered and the meat divided equally among members.

Pat's Party Spaghetti

This casserole will bring everyone back for seconds and even thirds.

Serves 12-14

2½ pounds ground round
2 16-ounce cans tomatoes
1 10-ounce can Ro-Tel Tomatoes and Green Chiles
8 ounces mushrooms, sliced
½ cup stuffed olives, chopped
1 2¼-ounce can ripe olives, sliced
1 medium onion, chopped
2 pounds American cheese, cubed
16 ounces spaghetti, cooked
1 pound bacon, cooked crisp
Salt and pepper to taste

Brown meat lightly in large skillet or stew pan. Drain any excess grease. Add tomatoes, Ro-Tel Tomatoes and Green Chiles, mushrooms, olives and onion. Mix thoroughly. Add cheese and spaghetti; crumble bacon over all. Mix gently and place in large baking dish or 3-quart casserole. Bake at 350° for 35-40 minutes. Serve with grated Parmesan cheese, crusty rolls and a green salad.

Reuben Casserole

The classic Reuben sandwich is transformed into a casserole in this unique recipe. The combination of flavors is delectable, and it is quick and easy to prepare.

Serves 6

2 cups sauerkraut, drained and rinsed
½ teaspoon caraway seed
½ pound corned beef, sliced thin
¼ cup Thousand Island dressing
2 large tomatoes, sliced
2 cups Swiss cheese, shredded
6 slices rye bread, crumbed
2 tablespoons butter or margarine, melted

Spread sauerkraut in bottom of an oiled 2-quart casserole. Sprinkle half of caraway seed over sauerkraut. Layer corned beef slices over sauerkraut and caraway, and drizzle dressing over all. Layer tomato slices and cheese over dressing. Toss bread crumbs and remaining caraway seeds in butter and spread over cheese. Bake at 400° for 25-30 minutes.

Main Dishes

"A MILE WIDE and a foot deep, too thin to plow and too thick to drink"—that's how many early El Pasoans referred to the Rio Grande, Texas' greatest river, the fourth longest in North America. Starting as a snow-fed mountain torrent in the Colorado Rockies, it empties into the Gulf as a sluggish, irregular stream. Along the way, it waters centuries-old Indian fields and carves out the canyons of Big Bend before finally creating the fertile delta of the Lower Rio Grande Valley. As befits such a complex river, the Rio Grande has known a number of names: Posoge ("river of great water"), Rio de las Palmas (because of the palm trees growing at its mouth), Rio Bravo (because of hostile Indians), Rio Turbio (because of its muddy-looking water).

Rio Grande Pot Roast

Serves 6-8

1 4-pound roast, chuck or rump
½ teaspoon black pepper
½ teaspoon ground cloves
½ teaspoon mace
½ teaspoon allspice
1 tablespoon salt
1 large onion, chopped
½ cup cooking oil
2 tablespoons lemon juice
1 tablespoon wine vinegar
1½ cups tomato juice
2 bay leaves
   Parsley for garnish

Dry meat by blotting with paper towels. Mix dry spices together and rub into cut surfaces of meat. Combine onion with ¼ cup oil, lemon juice, vinegar and tomato juice. Pour over meat, cover and refrigerate overnight. Remove meat from marinade and drain well. Place remaining ¼ cup of oil in large skillet over medium high heat. Sear roast on both sides. Lower heat, add marinade, onion and bay leaves; cover and simmer slowly for 3 hours. To serve, slice thin, spoon sauce from pan over slices and garnish with parsley.

Saucy Rump Slices from Lubbock

Serves 6-8

3 pound rump roast,
  cut 3½ inches wide
2 tablespoons oil, if needed
½ teaspoon salt
¼ teaspoon black pepper
3 ounces Cheddar cheese, grated
1 medium onion, chopped
1 4-ounce can sliced mushrooms,
  drained
1 15-ounce can tomato sauce
  Water

Trim excess fat from roast; place trimmings in a large skillet and cook over medium heat. Save rendered fat and discard cooked trimmings. Place roast on its side and cut into 3 or 4 1½-inch wide strips. Brown strips in rendered fat from trimmings. Add oil if necessary.

Remove strips to a cutting board and slice each one lengthwise three-fourths through to form a pocket. Sprinkle with salt and pepper. Stuff pockets with equal amounts of cheese, onion and mushrooms. Place stuffed strips back into skillet or a 4-quart baking dish and cover with tomato sauce. Add water to cover. Bake in a preheated 400° oven 45 minutes.

Remove to cutting board and slice with grain into ¼-inch slices. Arrange on serving platter, garnish with parsley, transfer pan sauce to a gravy bowl and serve.

Main Dishes

"GONE TO TEXAS" was written beside the names of a lot of desperate men who were fleeing from hanging or jail. As the Texas frontier had few lawmen to pursue them or judges to try them, these ruffians became increasingly bold and numerous, until early Texans were forced to form vigilante committees to protect their families and property.

Texas Stuff

A short-cut recipe to tasty eating.

Serves 8

2 pounds lean ground beef
1 large onion, chopped
2 10-ounce cans tomatoes
   and green chiles
1 1-ounce package chili mix
2 15-ounce cans ranch style beans
1 pound processed American
   cheese, cubed
1 cup light cream or half-and-half
1 large bag tortilla chips

Brown ground beef in a large skillet and drain. Add onion and cook briefly. Add tomatoes with chiles, chili mix and beans and simmer for 15 minutes. Add cheese and cream and simmer for 5 minutes. Pour over tortilla chips to serve.

This may also be used as a hearty appetizer by serving in a chafing dish and with a basket of tortilla chips for dipping.

Main Dishes

A TEXAS BARBECUE involves some kind of meat, or combination of meats, cooked slowly in a pit or on a special grill over mesquite, hickory or oak coals until just the right degree of smoked goodness is reached. Quite often it is an event of some magnitude and requires a number of helpers and advisors. The meat can be brisket, ribs, sausage, chicken, goat, lamb, pork or whatever is available.

Barbecued Ribs

This recipe may be used with the barbecue grill when you want to feed a small number of people.

Serves 4

3-4 pounds spareribs or country ribs
1 teaspoon salt
1 teaspoon black pepper

Sauce
1 cup salad oil
½ cup vinegar
2 tablespoons Worcestershire sauce
2 cloves garlic
2 tablespoons lemon juice
½ cup catsup (optional)

Mix salt and pepper and rub on all surfaces of ribs. Place ribs on a rack in roasting pan; add water to pan to almost touch rack. Place uncovered pan in a 450° oven for 30 minutes.

Combine sauce ingredients in a saucepan and simmer briefly. Place ribs over low coals and cook slowly 1½ hours, basting frequently with sauce. If you like a tomato-based sauce, add catsup to basting sauce during last 30 minutes of cooking.

Main Dishes

LULING WAS A SLEEPY little farm town until Edgar B. Davis's persistent search for oil brought in the gusher called Rios No. 1 in 1922. Mr. Davis had no family, and he used his wealth to endow the Luling Foundation Farm and various projects in Luling. Luling is also known for its annual Watermelon Thump, which pays tribute to 80,000 acres of watermelon grown in the area. Top watermelons are auctioned as a highlight of the Thump, with the champion melon bringing as much as $2,000.

Glazed Country Ham

Serves 12

10-12 pound ham
  1 cup orange juice
  1 cup brown sugar
  1 cup bourbon
  1 tablespoon ground cloves

Place ham in a heavy-duty plastic bag. Mix remaining ingredients together and pour over ham. Close bag and refrigerate overnight.

To bake ham, remove from bag, reserving marinade. Place ham in roasting pan and bake at 325° for 2 hours. Remove skin from ham, score fat in 1-inch diamonds and insert a clove in each diamond. Baste with marinade sauce, and bake for 1 more hour.

Main Dishes

THEY DON'T MAKE MEN like Sam Houston anymore. At 16, Houston ran off to live with the Cherokee Indians rather than clerk in the village store. A hero in the War of 1812. Houston next became a lawyer, then a politician. Congressman by 1823 and Governor of Tennessee by 1827, Houston resigned as governor in 1829 after his bride of three months left him. He headed west to rejoin his Cherokee brothers for another six years as a businessman and diplomat. Houston first visited Texas in 1832 as an Indian agent but didn't actually settle down here until 1835, in Nacogdoches. By March 1836, he was commander-in-chief of the Texas Army; by September 1836, the Republic's first elected President. Sam Houston served twice as president of the new Republic of Texas, as U.S. Senator from Texas and, finally, as Governor of Texas. He is the only person to ever serve as Governor of two different states and as head of a foreign government.

Skillet Fried Rice with Ham

This is an easy and delicious way to use leftover ham.

Serves 4

1⅓ cups raw rice
1½ cups cooked ham, cubed
 1 medium onion, chopped
 ½ cup chopped green pepper
 ½ cup sliced celery
 2 tablespoons oil
    Salt and pepper to taste
 2 tablespoons soy sauce
 2 eggs

Cook rice according to directions on package for firm texture; cool. Place ham, onion, green pepper, celery and oil in a large skillet; saute until vegetables are glossy. Add salt and pepper, mixing well. Add rice and soy sauce, and stir. Break eggs into rice mixture and cook over medium heat, stirring constantly, until eggs are set.

Main Dishes

NOWADAYS about all we use charcoal for is barbecueing. At the turn of the century, however, thousands of Texans depended on charcoal stoves for heat in the winter as well as for cooking. Most of San Antonio's charcoal supply came from "Charcoal City," the name given the settlement of charcoal burners and cedar choppers who lived along the Guadalupe River above New Braunfels. They chopped down the abundant stands of cedar and oak, slow-burned the wood down to charcoal, then hauled it by wagon to San Antonio.

Grilled Pork Chops

Pork chops are wonderful grilled over a charcoal fire to which some hickory chips or chunks of mesquite are added for that special taste.

Serves 4

4 loin pork chops, ¾-inch thick
½ cup salad oil
¾ cup cider vinegar
4 tablespoons Worcestershire sauce
2 tablespoons butter
2 tablespoons lemon juice
2 garlic cloves, minced
2 tablespoons dry mustard

Have market cut chops ¾-inch thick. Wipe chops and place in a shallow baking dish. Combine remaining ingredients in a saucepan and bring to a simmer. Pour over pork chops and let stand for 15-20 minutes. Remove chops from sauce, reserving sauce, and place on grill over medium coals. Cook 15 minutes on each side, basting occasionally with sauce. For additional flavor, add damp hickory chips or mesquite chunks to coals.

Loin of Pork with Wine Sauce

This is the aristocrat of pork roasts and the wine sauce makes it tender and moist. It is an elegant dish and does not require a lot of last-minute time and effort.

Serves 6-8

3 tablespoons oil
3-4 pounds boned pork loin
2 onions, chopped
2 tablespoons flour
2 cups chicken broth or bouillon
1 cup white wine
1 clove garlic, minced
1 bay leaf
1 teaspoon minced parsley
Salt and pepper
Parsley and spiced apple rings
for garnish

Heat oil in a large skillet and brown pork roast on all sides. Remove roast from skillet, add onion and cook until tender. Add flour; cook and stir until lightly browned. Add chicken stock, wine, garlic, bay leaf, minced parsley, salt and pepper. Cook and stir over low heat until sauce is blended.

Place browned loin in a small roasting pan; pour wine sauce over top. Cover and cook at 325° for 2-2½ hours, adding more stock if necessary. Remove loin to cutting board, cut in thin slices and return to sauce.

To serve, arrange on platter, wreath with parsley and garnish with red apple rings. Pass remaining sauce.

Main Dishes

TEX-MEX has been called the Texification of Mexican cooking. It probably began when street vendors in San Antonio offered tamales, chili and tacos for sale in the mid-1800's. A tortilla was the perfect way to serve whatever tasty meat or sauce was available, and beans and rice served on the side filled the hungriest cowboy. The Mexican skill in blending the zesty flavors of peppers and spices was learned by others, and a new dimension was added to Texas cooking.

Tex-Mex Carnitas

This dish of shredded pork wrapped in flour tortillas is a slightly different and delicious version of an enchilada.

Serves 6-8

1 3-5 pound pork roast
1 1¼-ounce package taco seasoning
1 cup water
1 4-ounce can green chiles, chopped
12 flour tortillas

Cook pork roast 3 hours at 325°. Cool. Shred meat, discarding any fat. Place shredded meat, taco seasoning, water and green chiles in a large saucepan and simmer over low heat for 2 hours.

When ready to serve, steam tortillas to soften. Place a generous portion of shredded pork mixture on each tortilla and fold over. Serve with refried beans, guacamole, shredded cheese, sour cream and finely chopped lettuce. Offer Pico de Gallo or picante sauce for extra zip.

Main Dishes

"LET THE BEER do the talking" is the advertising philosophy at the Spoetzl Brewery in Shiner, home of Shiner Beer. Founder Kosmas Spoetzl would ice down a keg of Shiner in the back of his Model T and hit the highways, plying farmers and travelers with healthy helpings of his *hopswasser*. These days you have to go to the brewery's hospitality room for free samples; but, for aficionados, that's a small inconvenience. Each Labor Day hundreds of bicyclists pedal 90 miles from Austin to drink Shiner and attend the big picnic at the local Catholic Church.

Fried River Catfish

Serves 4

3 tablespoons bacon drippings
4 tablespoons oil
½ cup cornmeal
6 tablespoons flour
1 teaspoon salt
   Dash of pepper
1 egg, slightly beaten
1 tablespoon water
4 catfish

Heat bacon drippings and oil in a large skillet. Combine cornmeal, flour, salt and pepper. Mix egg and water. Dip fish into egg, then into cornmeal mixture. Place in hot oil and fry at medium heat until golden brown on both sides.

Main Dishes

FOR ALMOST 20 YEARS, Captain "Brownie" Brown delighted shiploads of bird lovers and sightseers with his witty and informative commentary as he piloted the *MV Whooping Crane* through the marshes of the Aransas National Wildlife Refuge in search of the stately whooping cranes. In 1981 he was given the Texas Hospitality Award because of his ability to make travelers feel welcome. Shortly after receiving this recipe from Captain Brown, we learned of his death; and the loss makes the recipe even more special.

Captain Brownie's Red Snapper

Serves 6

1   small onion, chopped
1   clove garlic, minced
1   tablespoon vegetable oil
1   16-ounce can stewed tomatoes, mashed
½   teaspoon salt
    Dash of pepper
3   lemons, sliced
2   pounds red snapper fillets

Sauté onion and garlic in oil in medium saucepan. Add tomatoes, salt and pepper and simmer for 10 minutes. Place each fish portion on 2 lemon slices in a 13x9-inch glass baking dish. Place 2 more lemon slices on top of each fish portion and ladle cooked sauce over top of fish. Bake at 375° for 30 minutes or until fish flakes easily when tested with fork.

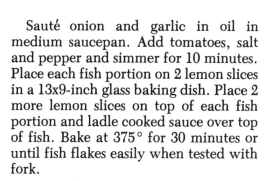

Yacht Club Snapper Throats

One of the featured items served at the Yacht Club Hotel and Restaurant in Port Isabel is this unusual dish. The throat of the Gulf red snapper is cut from the fish after the fillets and head have been removed.

Serves 6

2 pounds red snapper throats, scaled
½ cup butter, melted
1 teaspoon Season-all, or a good seasoned salt
½ teaspoon paprika

Break back bone of throats so they'll lie flat on a baking dish. Mix melted butter and Season-All or seasoned salt and apply generously to throats. Sprinkle with paprika. Cover with foil and broil in a 450° oven for 10 minutes or until fish is no longer opaque.

This recipe may be used with snapper fillets as well. Fillets need not be covered with foil.

Matagordo Oysters

It is claimed that Matagordo oysters are larger and have more flavor than oysters found elsewhere.

Serves 6

36 fresh oysters
6 slices bacon
½ onion
¼ cup celery, minced
1 cup chili sauce
1 teaspoon lemon juice
¼ cup horseradish

Open and drain oysters and place 2 in deep half of shell. Fry bacon until crisp, remove from pan, drain and crumble. Add onion and celery to bacon fat in skillet and cook until soft. Add chili sauce, lemon juice and horseradish to onion and celery mixture and heat. Spoon mixture over the oysters, top with crumbled bacon and bake at 400° for 10 minutes.

Main Dishes

JANE LONG, sometimes called the Mother of Texas, was a woman of great courage, resourcefulness and will to survive. When soldiers and settlers decided to abandon a small fort on Galveston Island, she chose to remain, believing her husband would return soon. With only her small daughter, a baby born during the ordeal and a young servant girl, she survived the terrible winter of 1822 by digging oysters from the frozen beach and firing the cannon to frighten away skulking Indians. After discovering that her husband had been killed, she had to find a way to support her family. She opened a boarding house in Brazoria and it became a gathering place for most of the movers and shapers of early Texas history.

Oyster Stew

Serves 6

2 cups oysters
2 tablespoons onion, chopped
3 tablespoons butter
4 cups milk, heated
   Salt and pepper to taste
   Minced parsley

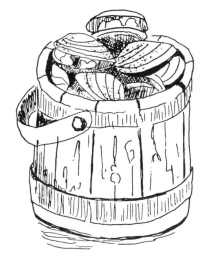

Chop oysters and onion. Melt butter in a medium saucepan, and sauté oysters and onions until oysters begin to curl. Pour hot milk over oyster mixture and mix. Salt and pepper to taste. Ladle into bowls and sprinkle minced parsley on top. Serve with oyster crackers.

Bay Shrimp with Rice

This could become your favorite shrimp recipe. It is a wonderful way to use the small salad shrimp—plentiful and inexpensive.

Serves 4

4 strips bacon, chopped
1 medium onion, chopped
½ cup green pepper, chopped
1½ teaspoon garlic, minced
1 cup rice, uncooked
¼ teaspoon thyme
1 tablespoon parsley, minced
¼ teaspoon cumin
1 pound raw shrimp, shelled and deveined
2 cups chicken stock
½ teaspoon salt
¼ teaspoon black pepper
Cayenne pepper to taste
1 teaspoon lemon juice

Cook bacon until almost crisp. Add onion, green pepper and garlic and saute until onions are soft. Turn heat to medium high and add rice. Cook, stirring constantly, for 2 minutes. Rice will be slightly browned. Lower heat, add thyme, parsley and cumin and stir. Add shrimp and 1 cup chicken stock. Cover and simmer for 5 minutes, or until shrimp turns pink. Add remaining chicken stock, salt, pepper, cayenne and lemon juice. Cover pan and simmer over low heat for 15 minutes. Remove from heat, stir gently with a fork, cover and let stand for another 5 minutes. Garnish with parsley and serve immediately.

Crown of Shrimp Ixtabay

When you have some big, beautiful Gulf shrimp and want to have a special dinner for two or three friends, this recipe is perfect!

Serves 2

12 large shrimp, uncooked
2 strips bacon
4 tablespoons butter, soft
1 clove garlic, minced
2 ounces white wine
    Juice from 2 lemons
    Salt and pepper to taste
    Parsley for garnish

Ixtabay Sauce
2 shallots, minced
1 clove garlic, minced
1 tablespoon butter
3 medium tomatoes, peeled
    and diced
4 sprigs cilantro, chopped
2 green onions, diced
1 tablespoon white wine
1 tablespoon capers, chopped
1 teaspoon lemon juice

Peel and devein shrimp, leaving tails intact. Butterfly by slicing lengthwise almost through. Pour boiling water over bacon to blanch. Place 6 shrimp in a circle, butterfly side down, with tails standing up in the center.

Wrap tails together tightly with strip of bacon and fasten with a wooden pick.

Mix soft butter and garlic and spread half on each crown. Pour wine and lemon juice over shrimp; cover loosely with foil and bake in a preheated 450° oven for 10-15 minutes.

Sauté shallots and garlic in butter until translucent. Add tomatoes and sauté 2 minutes. Add remaining ingredients and hold over very low heat until ready to serve.

When ready to serve, drain liquid from shrimp into sauce, mix and divide sauce onto two plates. Carefully place crown of shrimp over sauce, garnish and serve.

Main Dishes

GUESS YOU COULD CALL Jean Lafitte the "Father of Galveston" although the pirate chief had no such altruism in mind in 1817, when he established his *Maison Rouge* on the east end of Galveston Island. He just wanted a safe place to hang out between raids and a base for his attack on the rest of Texas. He even organized a government of sorts, but when he attacked U.S. ships in 1820, the Navy sailed against him and he fled in his favorite ship, the *Pride*, never to be seen again.

Culinarian Barbecued Shrimp

This prize recipe is from Galveston caterer Monica Reichenberger, who specializes in gourmet food prepared with a tropical flair.

Serves 6

2-3 pounds shrimp
 2 cups pineapple juice
 1 cup soy sauce
 1 cup safflower or peanut oil
 ½ cup molasses
 3 teaspoons Worcestershire sauce
 1 onion, cut in wedges

Peel and devein shrimp and place in a deep enameled or stainless steel bowl or pan. Combine pineapple juice, soy sauce, oil, molasses and Worcestershire sauce and pour over shrimp, making sure shrimp is covered. Add onion wedges, toss gently and refrigerate 1-2 hours.

Grill over medium coals and mesquite wood 4-6 minutes or until done. Serve with a platter of tropical fruits and crusty bread.

Main Dishes

THE TEXAS GULF COAST with its plentiful supply of shrimp, oysters, snapper, redfish and other goodies from the ocean is a mecca for Texans who love good eating. Yes Virginia, Texans do enjoy a lot of food other than chicken-fried steaks, barbecue and chili; and seafood ranks high on the list of favorites.

Coastal Bend Gumbo

This recipe is a winner of a Gumbo Cookoff in the Coastal Bend area. The roux is made with less flour than usual, and the contributors say curry powder is the magic ingredient.

Serves 20-25

¾ **cup shortening**
¾ **cup margarine**
¾ **cup flour**
2 **large green peppers, chopped**
8-10 **ribs celery, chopped**
3 **large onions, chopped**
4 **quarts water**
2 **teaspoons curry powder**
1 **teaspoon garlic powder**
1 **teaspoon gumbo file´**
6 **cups canned tomatoes, with liquid**
4 **cups okra, sliced**
2 **pounds shrimp, peeled**
1 **pound crabmeat**
  Tabasco, salt and pepper
6 **cups cooked rice, hot**

Heat shortening and margarine in a large, heavy kettle over medium heat. Add flour slowly, stirring constantly with a wooden spoon to make roux. Cook and stir until roux is a light golden brown. Add green peppers, celery and onion and cook for 10 minutes. Add water, seasonings, tomatoes and okra and simmer 15 minutes. Add shrimp and crabmeat and simmer 10 minutes. Add Tabasco, salt and pepper to taste.

To serve, place 4 tablespoons rice in each individual serving bowl and ladle gumbo over top.

Freezes well.

Main Dishes

OLD TIMERS claim Texas winters just aren't the same anymore, but then neither is the hunting. They say one winter it got so cold that Caddo Lake froze overnight, trapping thousands of slumbering geese. Come morning, they were flapping and squawking as they tried in vain to get loose. Before noon folks were coming from all over to harvest the honkers by the wagonload. They barely made a dent. The ice loosened enough the next day for the survivors to fly away.

Sherried Wild Duck

Serves 3-4

2 small ducks, plucked and cleaned
1 cup sherry
2 cups sauerkraut, drained
3 cups seasoned croutons
1 tablespoon seasoning salt
1 large onion, chopped
½ teaspoon red pepper
½ teaspoon black pepper

Place ducks and wine in a heavy plastic bag, closing bag tightly. Refrigerate overnight, turning ducks occasionally. When ready to cook, remove ducks from bag, reserving wine. Mix other ingredients and stuff into ducks. Pour reserved wine over ducks and cover loosely with large piece of foil. Bake at 300° for 1¾ hours. Remove foil and bake another 20 minutes.

Main Dishes

TEXAS WINES may not yet be as famous as those of California or France, but Texans have been making wine since the 1830's. German immigrants first tried to grow imported vines—unsuccessfully—before turning to the abundant supplies of native wild berries and grapes, especially mustang grapes. Mostly made for home consumption, the wine was long popular in German parts of Texas. In the late 1890's, when the vineyards of France were threatened by a root disease, the French wine industry was saved by disease-resistant Texas grapevines. So, there's a little bit of Texas in a lot of French wines.

Quail in Wine Sauce

Serves 4

8 quail
Salt
Lemon juice
½ cup oil
3 tablespoons onion, minced
1 cup chicken broth
½ cup white wine
1 cup sour cream

Rub quail with salt and lemon juice. Heat oil in a heavy skillet and brown quail on all sides. Remove from skillet and place in covered roasting pan. Mix onion and mushrooms in skillet drippings and saute until soft. Combine chicken broth, wine and sour cream with onions and mushrooms. Pour sauce over quail, cover and bake 1 hour at 350°.

Main Dishes

ENDANGERED by excessive hunting and trapping during the early 1900's, wild turkeys came under the protection of the Texas Parks and Wildlife Department, which began restocking suitable areas of the state with the game bird. Today the hunting season is carefully controlled, and the wary birds challenge the most seasoned hunter.

Wild Turkey with Pecan Stuffing

Wild turkey is dryer than domestic turkey, but is moist and tender when cooked in an oiled paper sack.

Serves 8-10

1 wild turkey, 8-10 pounds dressed	2 eggs, beaten
2 tablespoons butter or margarine	1½ cups pecans, chopped
1 large onion chopped or 1 cup green onions and tops, chopped	¼ cup fresh parsley, chopped
1 cup celery, diced	½ teaspoon salt
1 pound bulk pork sausage	Dash of black pepper
2 cups crumbled cornbread	¼ cup butter, melted
2 cups soft biscuit crumbs	2 tablespoons oil
	1 brown paper sack large enough to hold roasting pan

Blot turkey dry with paper towels. Melt butter in skillet over medium heat, add onion and celery and saute until tender. Add sausage and cook, stirring frequently, until no longer pink. Drain well. Add remaining ingredients, except for butter, and mix well. Spoon stuffing lightly into neck and body cavities of turkey, close bird and brush with melted butter. Place bird in a roasting pan. Oil inside of paper sack and carefully place pan in sack. Fold to seal. Roast in a preheated 450° oven for 30 minutes, being careful that sack does not touch heating elements. Lower heat to 375° and continue to cook for 2-2½ hours or until drumstick moves easily at the joint.

Horseshoe Mountain Ranch Buck Chili

This good venison recipe comes from a Hill Country ranch known for its beautiful setting, good food and warm hospitality.

Serves 10-12

2 pounds deer meat, coarsely ground
1 pound hamburger, coarsely ground
1 large onion, chopped
3 ribs celery, chopped
2 garlic cloves, minced
2 cups canned tomatoes
1 6-ounce can V-8 Juice
2 packages chili mix
2 tablespoons chili powder
½ teaspoon monosodium glutamate
1 teaspoon red pepper
Salt and pepper to taste
2 15-ounce cans kidney beans
Water if needed

Sear meat in a large skillet or Dutch oven until no longer pink. Add onion, celery and garlic and stir over medium heat until lightly browned. Add tomatoes, V-8 Juice and seasonings. Cover and simmer over low heat for 1 hour. Add beans and simmer 15 minutes. Add water if chili seems too thick.

Main Dishes

LYNDON BAINES JOHNSON, thirty-sixth President of the United States, loved the Texas Hill Country and returned to the LBJ Ranch near Stonewall whenever the pressures of office permitted. Today both the ranch (renamed the Lyndon Baines Johnson National Historic Park) and the LBJ State Park are open to the public. A tour of these properties provides some insight into the life of the former president, a chance to see a "living history" farm of the early 1900's, and a glimpse of Texas wildlife.

LBJ Ranch Deer Meat Sausage

This is a favorite at the LBJ Ranch. Mrs. Johnson recommends the finished product for a "late Sunday morning breakfast with scrambled eggs, hominy grits, hot biscuits and boiling-hot coffee."

Yields 200 pounds

½   deer
½   hog
25   ounces salt
20   ounces black pepper
8   ounces red pepper
2   ounces sage

Grind deer and hog meat and mix with remaining ingredients.

Cook with scrambled eggs or form patties and pan fry.

Main Dishes

THE Y. O. RANCH, which covers 50,000 acres of beautiful Texas Hill Country near Kerrville, has been owned by the Schreiner family since it was started by former Texas Ranger Captain Charles Schreiner in 1880. It is a true working ranch, and guests at its Dude Ranch have the thrill of sharing in a world of cowboys, campfires and covered wagons. The ranch boasts the nation's largest quality herd of longhorns and deserves credit for helping save the rangy breed from extinction. The numerous rare and exotic animals roaming the Y. O. range are a source of supply for many of the zoos throughout the United States. The Y. O. brand represents not only a ranch but a Texas way of life.

Bertie's Y. O. Ranch Chicken-Fried Venison

Y. O. Ranch cook Bertie Varner says this is the favorite meal served at the ranch and suggests serving it with good hot bread.

Serves 4-6

2 pounds venison, sliced ½-inch thick
1 13-ounce can evaporated milk
Water as needed
Salt, pepper, garlic powder and onion powder to taste
1 cup flour
Oil or shortening

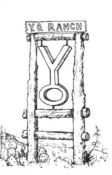

Beat venison slices with a board until thin and flat. Place in a shallow bowl, add evaporated milk and enough water to cover. Allow to stand 1 hour. Drain meat slightly, season to taste and dip in flour. Heat oil to 375°, add meat and fry until brown. Do not overcook or venison will become dry and tough. Serve with gravy made from pan drippings, leftover milk and flour.

Main Dishes

THE BLACK GOLD that gushed from the Spindletop well in 1901 signalled a major new industry for Texas. A young geologist from Beaumont, Patillo Higgins, had been convinced there was a vast oil reservoir in the area, but his attempts to tap it had resulted in dry wells. However, his persistence eventually paid off, and Spindletop gushed forth with an estimated 100,000 barrels of crude per day before finally being brought under control. Today, there are over 200,000 producing oil wells scattered throughout the state, and Texas is the nation's major petroleum producer.

Chiles Relleños

This recipe for green chiles stuffed with cheese is from The El Paso Chile Company.

Serves 3-4

1   10-ounce can whole green chiles
¾   pound Cheddar cheese, cut into 1-inch x ½-inch strips
    Salt
    Flour
4   eggs, separated
1   heaping teaspoon flour
    Oil

Drain chiles and pat dry. Remove seeds. Place strips of cheese inside chiles. Lightly salt chiles and roll in flour. Set aside. Beat egg whites until stiff. Beat egg yolks and add 1 heaping teaspoon flour. Fold egg yolk mixture into egg whites. Dip each chile in batter to completely coat. Pour oil into a large skillet to a depth of 2 inches and heat. Place chiles in hot oil and brown on both sides. Remove with slotted spoon, drain and serve while hot.

Main Dishes

EXCITING EL PASO, the western tip of Texas, is 775 miles from its opposite point on the eastern border of the state, Texarkana. El Paso and its sister city Juárez, across the Rio Grande, have long blended their cultures, languages and cuisines to form a unique and fascinating major population area of nearly one million people. Since the founding of the first Spanish missions in the area in the late 1600's, El Paso del Norte's historic and economic significance within the region has been enormous.

El Paso Enchiladas

Serves 4

8 corn tortillas
½ cup oil
1 cup Nena's Red Chile Sauce
  (see recipe below)

1½ cups Cheddar cheese, grated
1 large onion, chopped
4 eggs, fried
Shredded lettuce

Heat oil in 10-inch cast-iron skillet. Fry tortillas briefly in oil, drain on paper towels and cover to keep warm. Heat Nena's Red Chile Sauce in remaining oil. To assemble enchiladas, spread warm tortilla with a thin layer of sauce and place on serving plate, sprinkle with cheese and onions and top with another tortilla. Place in 150° oven while frying eggs. Place egg on top of stack and surround with shredded lettuce. Repeat process for each enchilada stack.

Nena's Red Chile Sauce
This is HOT! HOT! HOT!

6 large dried red chiles

3 cups water
1 teaspoon salt

Always use rubber gloves when handling chiles. Remove stems and tops from chiles and shake to remove seeds. Bring water to a boil in medium saucepan. Drop chiles in, push down with spoon, turn off heat and let stand in hot water 45 minutes. Puree chiles, ½ cup of chile water and salt in a blender for 30 seconds. Push chiles through strainer to remove skin and seeds. Chile sauce may be used on any food requiring a really *hot* sauce.

Pronto Green Beans with Sausages

This is one of the easiest main dishes you'll ever find. It's perfect for serving with corn bread and fresh sliced tomatoes.

Serves 4

4 cups cooked green beans
   with juice
1 12-ounce package smoke
   flavored link sausages
1 teaspoon Worcestershire sauce
½ teaspoon dry mustard
   Salt to taste.

Place beans and juice in a 2-quart saucepan. Cut sausages into bite-sized pieces and add to beans. Add Worcestershire sauce and mustard and simmer on low heat 20-25 minutes. Salt to taste.

Variation

If you're not in a hurry, use 1 pound fresh green beans, washed and snapped in bite-size pieces. Add sausages and cover with water. Bring to a boil, lower heat to simmer, and cook until beans are tender. Add Worcestershire sauce, mustard and salt and cook briefly. This dish is better cooked ahead and reheated when ready to serve.

Main Dishes

THE INSTITUTE OF TEXAN CULTURES in San Antonio tells the story of immigrants from all over the world who made Texas their home. Administered by the University of Texas, the Institute illustrates the rich cultural heritage of the state through exhibits of clothing, furniture, tools, music and books of some 25 nationalities and ethnic groups. An exciting way to view Texas history.

Slavic Oven Stew

This recipe is reprinted from **The Melting Pot**, *a cookbook of ethnic recipes collected by the Institute of Texan Cultures.*

Serves 8-10

10 medium onions, minced
8-10 large tomatoes, sliced
½ cup rice, uncooked
6-7 medium potatoes, pared and thinly sliced
5 lamb chops
5 pork chops
1 eggplant, pared and diced
6 green peppers
1 cup okra, diced
Salt and pepper to taste
2 tablespoons butter

Cover bottom of a roasting pan with onion. Arrange half of tomatoes on top of onion. Spread rice over tomatoes. Add potatoes, then chops, alternating lamb and pork. Seed peppers and slice into thin rings. Cover chops with eggplant and pepper slices. Add another layer of tomatoes. Cover with layer of okra. Sprinkle with salt and pepper and dot with butter. Cover and bake at 450° for 1 hour. Remove cover and continue cooking at 350° for 30 minutes or until done.

Main Dishes

EDWIN "GOOSE" RAMEY has lived in Dimmitt for the last 80 of his 94 years. He has distinguished himself as a pioneer rancher, farmer, beekeeper, after-dinner speaker, public official, meteorologist and notable authority on matters ranging from Panhandle history to the U.S. Treasury. He is best known, though, for his encyclopedic knowledge on the ways of Canadian wild geese.

Son-of-a-Gun Stew

Almost an entire unweaned calf goes into this authentic ranch stew, long enjoyed by cowboys for the special flavor that comes from the marrow gut filled with partially digested milk. This is Goose Ramey's version in his own words.

Serves 6-8

1 calf tongue
⅓ calf liver
1 oxtail soup bone
½ calf heart
Butcher steak
Marrow gut
1 hunk kidney fat about the size of a croquet ball
Brains
Sweetbreads

Boil the tongue for 30 minutes and scrape good. If you are not fond of tongue, you might put in only half or throw it away. That's what I do. Boil the liver for 30-40 minutes before adding to the stew. If you do not like liver taste, forget the liver. Boil the oxtail soup bone until meat is done and remove from bones. Cut tongue, liver, oxtail meat, heart, butcher steak and kidney fat into 1-inch hunks. Place in large kettle, cover with water and simmer for 3-4 hours. Add sweetbreads, brains, salt and pepper and simmer another 30-45 minutes.

VEGETABLES
AND SIDE DISHES

From Texas...

with love

Guacamole

Guacamole is used as a dip with tortilla chips, heaped on shredded lettuce as a salad or served as a side dish for many Tex-Mex meals. A good guacamole recipe is a must in any book about Texas cooking, and this one is superb.

Yields 1½ cups

2 large ripe avocados
1 tablespoon lime juice
1 medium tomato, skinned and finely chopped
2 tablespoons onion, minced
½ teaspoon ground coriander
½ teaspoon salt
1 tablespoon picante sauce (optional)

Peel avocados, remove pits and reserve one pit. Mash pulp with fork. Add lime juice, tomato, onion, coriander and salt. Add picante sauce if desired. Mix well. Place avocado pit on top of guacamole, cover and refrigerate; remove pit when ready to serve.

Marinated Black-Eyed Peas

Eating black-eyed peas on New Year's Day guarantees good luck for the entire year.

Yields 3 cups

1 15-ounce can black-eyed peas
¾ cup vegetable oil
⅓ cup cider vinegar
1 clove garlic, pressed
¼ cup onion, minced
½ teaspoon salt
¼ teaspoon black pepper

Drain peas and place in a medium bowl. Combine oil, vinegar, garlic, onion, salt and pepper and pour over peas. Cover and refrigerate 2 or 3 days. Serve as an appetizer or as a relish.

Vegetables and Side Dishes

BEEF PRICES being what they are these days, it's hard to imagine that just after the Civil War a cow's hide was worth more than the live cow. Hide and tallow factories lined Texas' major rivers and the Gulf Coast. At a plant near the coastal hamlet of Quintana, workers shucked off the hides and skidded the meat down chutes directly into the sea. So many sharks were attracted to the area that people were afraid to go swimming in the surf.

Barley-Almond Casserole

Serves 6

½ cup butter
2 medium onions, chopped
¾ pound mushrooms, chopped
1¼ cups pearl barley
1 small jar pimento
½ teaspoon salt
¼ teaspoon pepper
2 cups canned chicken broth
4 ounces slivered almonds

Melt butter in medium saucepan and saute onion and mushrooms. Add barley and cook until barley is a delicate brown. Add pimento, salt and pepper; mix. Put into a 2-quart casserole, add chicken broth and spread nuts on top. Cover and bake at 350° for 1½ hours.

Vegetables and Side Dishes

"COMMENT CA VAS?" is the traditional Cajun greeting for "How y'all go?" Just as distinctive as the Cajun accent in Southeast Texas and Louisiana are the delicious Cajun dishes — from banjo rice and beans to *jambalaya*, gumbo to *court bouillon*. And the Cajun accents and food are to be found at *fais do do* (all-night dance parties). *"Cajun"* is short for Acadian—the name of the French-speaking colonists who migrated to Louisiana rather than accept British rule in Canada.

Banjo Rice and Beans

There's a taste of Louisiana in this combination.

Serves 8

2½ pounds ham with bone
1 pound dry pinto beans, washed and picked over
1 large onion, grated
1 green pepper, grated

2 cloves garlic, chopped
4 tablespoons bacon drippings
Pinch of sugar
Salt to taste
1 pound long grain rice

Cover ham with water and simmer 1 hour. Drain. Remove ham from bone, trim fat and cut into 2-inch cubes. Return to saucepan, add 1½-2 cups fresh water, bring to a simmer and cook until ham cuts with a fork.

Place beans in large kettle and cover with water to depth of 1 inch above top of beans. Bring to boil over high heat. Lower heat; add onion, green pepper, garlic and bacon drippings. Add ham with its water and simmer, stirring occasionally, for 2-3 hours or until beans are tender. Add sugar and salt just before removing from heat.

About 30 minutes before serving, cook rice according to directions on package.

To serve, spoon beans and ham over rice. Accompany with hot cornbread and sausage. Pass Louisiana hot sauce, salt and pepper.

Vegetables and Side Dishes

CHARLIE GOODNIGHT invented it, but that's not why we call it the chuck wagon. The chuck wagon evolved with the trail drives. In early Texas cattle drives, each trail hand carried his own food. As the drives grew larger and longer, trail bosses began to take a cook along, and a pack horse or ox cart carried the outfit's "chuck" (grub). After the Civil War, cowmen began to adapt wagons to their needs, but it took Goodnight to set the standard. He rebuilt a government surplus wagon with bois d'arc wood and iron axles and put a chuck box on the end. The chuck box, filled with "eatin' irons," a keg of sourdough, salt pork and dried beans, molasses and bottle of whiskey (for snakebite only) also served as cupboard, table and medicine cabinet.

Chuck Wagon Beans

Serves 12

4 cups pinto beans
1 pound salt pork or ham hocks
2 medium onions, chopped
2 tablespoons sugar
3 teaspoons chili powder
6 ounces tomato paste
   Salt to taste

Wash beans and soak overnight. Drain, place in a large kettle or Dutch oven and cover with water. Add remaining ingredients, except for salt. Simmer 3-4 hours, stirring occasionally. Add salt to taste and more water if needed. Cook another hour, or until beans are tender.

Vegetables and Side Dishes

JUDGE ROY BEAN, saloon keeper in a construction camp near Langtry, was the self-proclaimed "Law West of the Pecos." Bean knew nothing about the law, but he dealt out frontier justice with the help of a law book and six-shooter, both at hand during a trial. Although his interpretation of the law was versatile, Bean was not a hanging judge. Instead, he often fined the accused his guns and horse and ran him out of town. Prior to his judging days, Bean lived in San Antonio in a district still called Beanville. One day a customer complained about finding minnows in milk purchased from Bean's dairy. Water down his milk? Never! Bean explained the minnows were there because his cows had been drinking from the San Antonio River.

Southwestern Baked Beans

These beans are baked long and slow for a wonderful old-fashioned flavor.

Serves 12

1¼ cups dried navy beans
1¼ cups dried pinto beans
1¼ cups dried baby lima beans
 Water to cover
 1 teaspoon salt
 ½ pound salt pork, cut in chunks
 2 small onions, chopped
 ½ teaspoon black pepper
 1 tablespoon dry mustard
 1 tablespoon ground ginger
 ½ cup brown sugar
 ½ cup light molasses

Wash beans, cover with water and soak overnight. Place in a 4-quart saucepan, add salt, bring to a boil and simmer 15 minutes. Drain, reserving liquid. Place ¼ of the salt pork in the bottom of a 5-quart casserole or bean pot. Cover with alternating layers of onions and beans. Press remaining chunks of salt pork into top layer of beans. Combine reserved liquid with remaining ingredients in a saucepan, bring to a boil, and pour over beans. Add water to cover, if needed. Cover and bake at 250° for 6-7 hours.

Broccoli with Caper Sauce

Capers and dill do wonderful things for broccoli. The sauce should be made and the broccoli cooked several hours before serving.

Serves 6

1   bunch broccoli
½   teaspoon salt
    Water to cover broccoli
1   teaspoon lemon juice
1   cup mayonnaise
1   tablespoon wine vinegar
1   tablespoon lemon juice
1   tablespoon onion, minced
1   tablespoon capers, minced
1   teaspoon dill weed
1   egg yolk, hard boiled

Cut off large leaves and most of stalks of broccoli. Wash well. Place broccoli in saucepan, cover with water, add salt and lemon juice and bring to boil. Cook, uncovered, for 15 minutes or until tender. Drain and cool. Place remaining ingredients except egg yolk in blender and blend at low speed for 15 seconds. Refrigerate. Spoon over broccoli just before serving. Sieve egg yolk over top for garnish.

Vegetables and Side Dishes

THE SUNDAY HOUSES of Fredericksburg were built by ranchers and rural families to use when they came to town for marketing and business on Saturday and church on Sunday. Most were built around the turn of the century and were usually one room structures with a lean-to kitchen and a half-story sleeping loft reached by an outside stairway or ladder. A few have been preserved or restored, and they have become major attractions in this fascinating town.

Rotkohl (Red Cabbage)

The sturdy band of German pioneers who settled in Fredericksburg in 1846 brought their recipes with them and today's Fritztown cooking reflects this heritage.

Serves 8-10

2 tablespoons margarine
1 medium onion, chopped
1 medium head red cabbage, shredded
2 tart apples, diced
4 tablespoons sugar
Salt and pepper
½ cup water
4 tablespoons white vinegar

Melt margarine in a large saucepan, add onion and sauté until tender. Add cabbage, apples, sugar, salt, pepper and water and bring to a boil. Cover and cook gently for 10 minutes. Uncover, stir well, add vinegar and mix. Cover and simmer 15-20 minutes.

Vegetables and Side Dishes

FOOD and weather have long gone hand in hand as popular topics of conversation in Texas. A bumper crop year like 1882 prompted Blanco's E.C. "Uncle Clem" Hines to observe, "Some years Texas floats in grease." But the drought of 1886 prompted another farmer to reminisce, "The corn crop was sorter short that year. We had corn for dinner one day and Paw ate 15 acres of it."

Baked Barbecued Corn

Serves 6

6 ears corn, with husks
3 tablespoons butter or margarine
1 teaspoon chili powder
½ teaspoon onion powder
½ teaspoon salt
Dash of black pepper
2 tablespoons water

Pull husks carefully from corn so that husk remains attached to the bottom of corn ear. Remove silk from corn.

Melt butter in small saucepan, add seasonings and stir. Brush butter mixture on ear of corn. Pull corn husks up to cover corn and tie with string. Place in 13x9-inch glass baking dish, sprinkle with water, cover with foil and bake at 350° for 30 minutes.

Grilled Barbecued Corn

Prepare corn as in recipe above, to the point of placing corn in the baking dish. Instead, place corn directly on the grill over a medium hot charcoal fire. Cook for 30-40 minutes, turning every few minutes. Remove husks, which will be brown and dry, before serving.

Corn-Stuffed Fresh Tomatoes

Serves 6

6 medium tomatoes
¼ cup celery, chopped
¼ cup onion, chopped
4 teaspoons butter
¼ cup Cheddar cheese, shredded
1 12-ounce can white shoepeg corn, drained
1 tablespoon dried basil
1 tablespoon fresh parsley, chopped
½ teaspoon pepper
½ teaspoon salt

Cut ½-inch slice from top of each tomato. Carefully remove pulp so that shell of tomato remains intact. Drain any juice left in shell. Chop pulp and set aside.

Sauté celery and onion in butter until tender. Add tomato pulp and remaining ingredients and stir well. Spoon mixture into tomato shells and place in flat baking dish. Bake at 350° for 20-25 minutes.

Shoepeg Corn with Green Chiles

Serves 8

1 8-ounce package cream cheese, softened
¼ pound butter, softened
2 cloves garlic, minced
1 4-ounce can diced green chiles, drained
3 16-ounce cans white shoepeg corn, drained

Stir softened cream cheese and butter together. Add remaining ingredients and mix. Pour into 2-quart casserole and bake at 325° for 30 minutes.

Vegetables and Side Dishes

IT WAS THE DAY after San Jacinto, and a captured Santa Anna stood humbled before a triumphant Sam Houston.

"You cannot hope to conquer a people whose General and men can march three days on a ration of one ear of corn," Houston said as he held up a single dry ear, only partially consumed. The ragtag Texian troops crowded around and cheered.

"Give us that ear of corn," one of them shouted. "We'll plant it and call it Houston corn." Houston gladly distributed the kernels, but added: "Do not call it Houston corn. Call it San Jacinto corn, for then it will remind you of your own bravery." It was done, and tradition has it that thousands of tassled acres today boast pedigrees that trace back to that San Jacinto ear.

San Jacinto Corn

Serves 4

6 ears corn
6 tablespoons butter
2 tablespoons green pepper, chopped
2 tablespoons pimento, diced
½ teaspoon salt
¼ teaspoon black pepper

Husk corn and remove silk. Slice corn kernels from cobs with sharp knife. Use back of knife to scrape milk from cobs. Heat butter in skillet, add corn and corn milk and cook 3-4 minutes. Add green pepper, pimento, salt and pepper and simmer another 4 minutes.

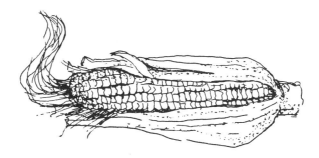

Vegetables and Side Dishes

YOU WON'T FIND his name on any patent, but John Grenninger of Austin invented and was using barbed wire more than a decade before the first patent for it was issued. A foundry worker, Grenninger constructed his prototype wire in 1857 by twisting two smooth wires tightly together and inserting sharp pieces of iron or glass at regular intervals between the wires. He nailed this pointed strand along the top of the wooden fence which surrounded his orchard and garden. His invention was effective—neighbors soon complained about the cuts their livestock were suffering, and many a boy was snagged as he tried to escape with Grenninger's peaches and watermelons. Grenninger's murder, five years after he first strung his invention, meant he never realized the impact barbed wire would have on ranching, farming and the entire economy of Texas.

Garlic Cheese Grits

Serves 8

4 cups water
1 teaspoon salt
1 cup grits
½ cup butter
4 eggs, well beaten
½ pound Cheddar cheese, grated
1 large clove garlic, minced
Dash of Tabasco sauce

Bring water to boil in a medium saucepan. Add salt and grits and cook, stirring, until water is absorbed. Add butter, eggs, cheese, garlic and Tabasco sauce; mix well. Pour into a buttered 2-quart baking dish and bake for 1 hour at 325°.

Green Beans with Almonds

Serves 6

2 tablespoons sliced almonds
¾ cup celery, sliced
1 clove garlic, minced
2 tablespoons butter
¾ cup chicken broth
1 tablespoon cornstarch
2 tablespoons soy sauce
2 16-ounce cans French-style
   green beans, drained

Sauté almonds, celery and garlic in butter until celery is tender. Add chicken broth, cornstarch and soy sauce; simmer until thickened. Add green beans, stir to mix and heat thoroughly.

German Green Beans

Serves 6

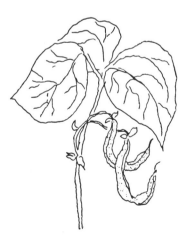

4 slices bacon
1 onion, thinly sliced
2 tablespoons flour
1 tablespoon sugar
½ teaspoon salt
¼ cup vinegar
¼ cup water
4 cups cooked or canned green
   beans, drained

Fry bacon until crisp; remove from skillet, leaving drippings. Add onions and cook until tender. Add flour, sugar, salt, vinegar and water. Mix well and simmer until slightly thickened. Add beans and cook for 5 minutes. Crumble bacon on top just before serving.

Vegetables and Side Dishes

WANT TO LIVE to be 100? Old-time Texas rancher Isom Like offered the following *remedio* on his century birthday: "Live temperately in food and drink. Try to get your beefsteak three times a day fried in taller. Taller is mighty healing, and there's nothing like it to keep your stummick greased up and in good working order."

Taller—beef tallow—was a substitute for both lard and butter. Sizzling-hot tallow mixed with molasses was a favorite cowboy dessert.

Elaine's Black-Eyed Peas and Okra

This tasty Texas recipe comes from out Dripping Springs way.

Serves 4

2 cups black-eyed peas with snaps, cooked
½ cup liquid from peas
1 medium onion, thinly sliced
1 medium tomato, peeled and sliced
2 cups okra, sliced
Salt and pepper to taste

Layer ingredients in order in a 2-quart saucepan. Cook over low heat for 10-15 minutes, until vegetables on top layers are steamed.

Onion Pie

Serves 6

1 cup saltine crackers, finely crushed
½ cup butter, melted
2 cups onion, thinly sliced
⅔ cup milk
2 eggs, slightly beaten
½ cup Cheddar cheese, shredded

Combine cracker crumbs and butter; mix well. Press firmly into 8-inch pie plate to make crust.

Sauté onion in bacon drippings over medium heat until glossy. Turn into cracker crust. Mix milk, eggs and cheese and pour over onion. Bake at 350° for 30 minutes.

Potato Pancakes with Applesauce

This old favorite is made easy by using frozen hashbrowns. Of course, if you're up for grating potatoes, it will be even better.

Serves 4

2 eggs, beaten
1 tablespoon flour
2 tablespoons milk
¼ teaspoon salt
1 tablespoon minced onion
1 12-ounce package frozen shredded hashbrown potatoes, thawed
3 tablespoons oil
3 tablespoons oil
Applesauce

Mix eggs, flour, milk, salt and onion in large bowl. Add thawed potatoes and mix. Heat oil in large heavy skillet. Drop heaping tablespoon of potato mixture into hot shortening and flatten with spoon. Repeat for each pancake. Cook until golden brown on bottom, turn once to brown other side. The edges will be crips and lacy. Serve with applesauce.

Potatoes with Creamy Dill Sauce

This recipe is an example of the good Czechoslovakian cooking found in the town of West.

Serves 6-8

2 pounds potatoes
4 tablespoons margarine or butter
4 tablespoons flour
½ teaspoon salt
4 tablespoons finely chopped fresh dill
1 cup light cream
1 cup milk

Peel and quarter potatoes and cook in salted water until tender. While potatoes are cooking, melt margarine or butter in saucepan over low heat. Add flour, salt and dill, stirring constantly. When smooth, cook for a few seconds. Add cream and milk gradually to butter mixture, stirring constantly until sauce thickens. Drain potatoes when done, transfer to serving bowl, and cover with creamy dill sauce.

Vegetables and Side Dishes

THE CONFEDERATE AIR FORCE is dedicated to collecting, restoring and preserving the combat aircraft of World War II. The Flying Museum of the Confederate Air Force in Harlingen houses the Ghost Squadron, made up of 120 aircraft and related items from the years 1939-45. Each October, the drama of the 4-day "Airsho" brings thousands to see these planes fly exhibitions and simulated combat missions. For many it is a time to relive an incredible era of their lives and to pay tribute to the men and women who built, serviced and flew these planes.

Culpeper's Angels' Favorite Potato Salad

The mythical commander of the Confederate Air Force is Colonel Jethro E. Culpeper, who has served in every war since 1776.

Serves 25 or more

10 pounds Irish potatos, boiled, diced, and cooled
2 large onions, chopped
1 12-ounce jar sweet relish
1 cup celery, chopped
1 cup salad dressing
1 tablespoon salt
1 tablespoon sugar
⅓ cup vinegar
1 4-ounce jar pimentos, chopped
6 hard-boiled eggs, chopped

Combine potatoes, onion, relish and celery; set aside. Combine salad dressing, salt, sugar, vinegar and pimentos and add to potato mixture. Mix well. Refrigerate several hours. Add egg just before serving.

Vegetables and Side Dishes

A FRONTIER TRADING POST established by Colonel Henry L. Kinney in 1839 was the beginning of the city of Corpus Christi. In 1852, Colonel Kinney, ever the town booster, sponsored a Lone Star Fair with fireworks, horse races, stock shows and bullfights. Today, people flock to Corpus Christi to enjoy the beaches, the food and an atmosphere of fun.

Barbecued Rice

This is cooked on the grill with the meat and is delicious.

Serves 4-6

1⅓ cups Minute Rice
2 tablespoons onion, chopped
½ teaspoon salt
Dash of pepper
¼ cup stuffed olives, sliced
1 teaspoon Worcestershire sauce
1 teaspoon prepared mustard
2 tablespoons chili sauce
2 tablespoons butter
1⅓ cups water

Press two large squares heavy duty aluminum foil into deep mixing bowl. Put Minute Rice and onion into foil-lined bowl. Mix remaining ingredients together and pour over rice and onion. Pull corners of foil together, fold and seal tightly to form a pouch. Place on grill and cook 20-25 minutes. Open pouch, fluff gently with a fork and serve.

Vegetables and Side Dishes

BEAUTIFUL TYLER is famous for its azaleas in the spring and its roses in the fall. More than half of all the rose bushes grown in the United States originated from the large commercial fields near Tyler.

Browned Rice with Peas

Serves 8

2　tablespoons butter
¾　cup rice, uncooked
1　8-ounce can sliced mushrooms,
　　Water
1　chicken bouillon cube
1　10-ounce package frozen peas,
　　partially thawed
2　tablespoons butter
¼　cup onion, chopped
1　tablespoon soy sauce

Heat butter in a large skillet. Add rice and cook over medium heat until golden brown, stirring frequently. Drain mushrooms, reserving liquid. Add enough water to mushroom liquid to yield 2 cups. Stir liquid and bouillon cube into rice. Cover and simmer over low heat for 15 minutes. Mix in the frozen peas and simmer another 10 minutes, or until rice and peas are tender. Melt butter in a small pan, add onions and mushrooms, and stir until lightly browned. Add mushrooms, onion and soy sauce to the rice mixture and toss lightly with fork to mix. Serve immediately.

Cheddar Squash Bake

Serves 8-10

8-10 medium yellow squash, sliced
1 teaspoon salt
1 cup sour cream
2 egg yolks, beaten
2 tablespoons flour
2 egg whites, stiffly beaten
1½ cups shredded Cheddar cheese
4 slices bacon, cooked
1 tablespoon butter, melted
⅓ cup dry bread crumbs

Steam or boil squash in small amount of water until tender. Drain and sprinkle with salt. Mix sour cream, egg yolks and flour. Fold into egg whites. Oil a 2-quart casserole. Layer half squash, egg mixture and cheese and crumble bacon on top. Repeat layers of squash, egg mixture and cheese. Combine butter and bread crumbs and sprinkle over cheese. Bake uncovered at 350° for 20-25 minutes or until bubbly and lightly browned.

French Squash with Almonds

*This recipe, from **The Melting Pot**, the cookbook of the Institute of Texan Cultures, was prepared by the French who settled in Texas.*

Serves 4-6

1 pound zucchini or yellow squash
¼ cup flour
Salt and pepper
5 tablespoons butter or margarine
½ cup almond halves
½ cup light cream

Wash the squash and cut into ½-inch slices. Toss slices in flour seasoned with salt and pepper. Melt butter in a frying pan, add squash and fry until golden on both sides. Drain and arrange slices in a serving dish. Fry almonds slowly in butter until they begin to brown. Drain and sprinkle over squash. Heat cream gently and pour over squash. Season with salt and pepper to taste and serve piping hot.

"TEJAS" (pronounced "tay-hahs") is an Indian word meaning "friends." Early Spanish missionaries found the Tejas Indians, known as "the friendly ones," in one of the areas they traveled through. They began to call that general area "the land of the Tejas." English-speaking settlers changed the spelling and pronunciation to "Texas" and it eventually became the name of the entire state.

Deep-Fried Zucchini

Don't like zucchini? This recipe works equally well with mushrooms.

Serves 4

3 medium zucchini
1 cup flour
2 teaspoons baking powder
1 teaspoon salt
½ cup corn meal
¼ teaspoon black pepper
½ teaspoon garlic powder
1 teaspoon seasoned salt
1 cup milk
1 egg, beaten
3 tablespoons oil

Sweet & Sour Sauce
¼ cup currant jelly
¼ cup prepared mustard

Cut zucchini into ¼-inch slices. Set aside. Combine dry ingredients. Combine milk, egg and oil and mix with dry ingredients.

Pour oil into a saucepan to a depth of at least 1½ inches. Heat oil to 375°. Dip zucchini in batter to coat; shake slightly to remove excess batter. Drop into hot oil and fry until golden brown. Remove with a slotted spoon, place in a paper towel-lined baking dish and hold in a 200° oven until all slices are fried.

To prepare sauce, bring jelly and mustard to a simmer in saucepan. Serve in a small bowl surrounded by Deep-Fried Zucchini.

Sweet Potato Bake with Pecan Topping

Serves 6

3 cups sweet potatoes,
  cooked and mashed
¼ cup milk
⅓ cup butter, melted
1 teaspoon vanilla
2 eggs, beaten
½ teaspoon salt

Topping
1 cup pecans, chopped
1 cup brown sugar
3 tablespoons flour
⅓ cup butter, melted
1 cup coconut, optional

Mix mashed sweet potatoes, milk, butter, vanilla, eggs and salt. Spoon into a 1½-quart oiled casserole.

Combine topping ingredients and sprinkle over sweet potatoes. Bake at 375° for 25 minutes.

Coconut Yam Balls

Serve these around a whole ham as an attractive garnish.

Serves 6

4 medium yams, cooked
1 teaspoon salt
2 tablespoons butter
8 marshmallows, cut in half
1 cup shredded coconut

Combine yams, salt and butter and mash until smooth. Form mashed yams into balls with marshmallow halves as the center. Roll balls in coconut and bake at 350° for 10 minutes, or until a delicate brown.

Garden Stir-Fry

This favorite way to prepare vegetables may be varied according to what is available.

Serves 4

1½ tablespoons oil
1 large carrot, sliced
1 large rib celery, sliced
½ cup onion, sliced
1 zucchini, sliced
1 cup broccoli flowerets
½ cup fresh mushrooms, sliced
¼ cup chicken broth
Salt and pepper to taste

Heat the oil in a large skillet until hot but not smoking. Add carrot, celery and onion and stir while cooking for about 2 minutes. Add zucchini, broccoli and mushrooms. Stir until coated. Add chicken broth, cover and cook for 5 minutes. Season and serve.

Dill Cucumbers in Sour Cream

Serves 6

2 cucumbers
1 onion, thinly sliced
¼ cup sour cream
1 tablespoon vinegar
1 teaspoon sugar
½ teaspoon salt
1 tablespoon fresh dill, finely chopped

Wash and dry cucumbers and score sides with the tines of a fork. Slice and combine with remaining ingredients. Refrigerate 3-4 hours.

Macaroni and Cheese Supreme

This new treatment of an old favorite is creamy and simply delicious.

Serves 8

1¾ cups elbow macaroni, cooked	2 cups American cheese shredded
2 cups small curd cottage cheese	¾ teaspoon salt
1 cup sour cream	1½ tablespoons butter
1 egg, slightly beaten	¼ cup bread crumbs
3 tablespoons onion, minced	

Mix all ingredients except butter and bread crumbs and pour into a 2-quart greased casserole. Melt butter in a small saucepan, add bread crumbs and mix. Sprinkle over macaroni cheese mixture. Bake at 350° for 45 minutes.

Apple Escallop

Try this with roast pork or baked ham during harvest season when good tart apples are available.

Serves 6-8

½ cup sugar
½ cup brown sugar
¼ cup flour
8 cups apples, peeled, cored and cut into chunks
¼ cup melted butter
¼ cup hot water

Combine sugars, flour and apples. Add melted butter and mix. Turn out into a 2-quart buttered casserole. Pour water over apples, cover and bake 30-40 minutes. Remove cover and bake another 15 minutes until slightly browned.

NOTED FRONTIERSMAN and Indian fighter William A. A. "Bigfoot" Wallace had an appetite as big as his legendary reputation. At 6'2" and 240 pounds, Bigfoot could pack away the groceries, especially if he hadn't eaten in three or four days. Once while driving the mail from San Antonio to El Paso, Bigfoot was attacked by Apaches, who left him afoot, foodless, and a 3-day walk from the nearest house. When Wallace came to that house he bolted down 27 raw eggs and hit the trail again in search of a square meal.

Caper Stuffed Eggs

These tender stuffed eggs are a delicious change from the usual deviled eggs.

Serves 4

4 eggs
1 tablespoon sour cream
1 teaspoon dijon mustard
1 tablespoon capers, finely chopped
1 tablespoon ripe olives, finely chopped
   Salt and pepper to taste
1 teaspoon celery salt
   Parsley for garnish

Place eggs in cold water in a stainless steel or enamel pan. Bring water to a boil, lower heat and boil gently for 4 minutes. Remove pan from heat, cover and allow to stand 10 minutes.

Drain and fill pan with cold water. When eggs are cool, peel and slice lengthwise. Remove yolks and put them through a sieve into a small bowl. Add remaining ingredients and mix until blended. Fill whites with yolk mixture and garnish with parsley.

Mandarin Oranges in the Whole

These little oranges are pretty enough for a party or luncheon and fun to make.

Serves 4

2 11-ounce cans Mandarin oranges, drained
1 envelope unflavored gelatin

1 cup orange juice

Spread Mandarin orange sections on paper towels and blot dry. Dissolve gelatin in orange juice over low heat. Assemble 8 or 9 orange sections in the palm of your hand so they form a complete orange. Hold loosely over a bowl and spoon gelatin mixture over each section to coat thoroughly. Squeeze segments together very gently so orange appears whole and place in 2-inch muffin cup. (This is a smaller muffin tin than usual.) Continue to form oranges and coat with gelatin until all of whole segments are used. Spoon more gelatin over and around oranges and refrigerate at least 3 hours. Any broken segments and the remaining gelatin mixture may be combined and refrigerated. Serve the complete oranges with the following sauce.

Currant Sauce

1 6-ounce jar currant jelly
⅔ cup orange juice
   Juice of 1 lemon

¼ teaspoon cinnamon
Zest from 4 oranges
Grand Marnier or Curaçao to taste

Place jelly, orange juice, lemon juice and cinnamon in a small saucepan and heat until jelly melts. Using a vegetable peeler, pare thin orange portion of peeling from oranges and cut into thin strips. Stir into the jelly mixture and add liqueur. Chill. When ready to serve, spoon sauce over top of the oranges and serve surrounded by parsley. Allow 2 oranges per serving.

SWEETS
AND TREATS

From Texas...

with love

Sweets and Treats

DWIGHT DAVID EISENHOWER was born in Denison, Texas, but neither he nor the people of Denison knew it until he became a national figure. A Denison school principal remembered rocking a little Eisenhower baby and wrote the general's mother to see if the baby could have been the famous general. A search of the records proved fruitful, and Denison residents proudly restored the house in which the thirty-fourth President of the United States was born.

Fay's Fresh Apple Cake

A special lady from Denison remembers her friends and relatives on their birthdays by baking them a favorite cake. This one is requested more often than any other in her extensive recipe collection.

Serves 12-16

3 eggs, beaten	½ teaspoon salt
2 cups sugar	1 teaspoon vanilla
1½ cups cooking oil	2 cups apples, chopped
3 cups flour	1 cup pecans or walnuts,
1 teaspoon soda	finely chopped

Mix eggs and sugar together. Add oil and beat until smooth. Sift flour, soda and salt together and gradually add to egg mixture. Stir in vanilla and mix well. Fold in apples and nuts. Pour batter into oiled bundt pan and bake at 325° for 1-1½ hours. Test at end of 1 hour by inserting a toothpick to see if it comes out clean. Continue baking if necessary. Allow cake to cool in pan for 20 minutes. Remove from pan and top with glaze.

Glaze

Yield 1 cup

1 cup confectioner's sugar	2 tablespoons milk

Sift confectioner's sugar and mix with milk until smooth. Spread glaze while cake is still warm.

Cherry Cheesecake Supreme

Cheesecake topped with a red cherry sauce is a perfect way to end dinner with a flourish.

Serves 12

1¾ cups graham cracker crumbs
½ cup sugar
¼ cup pecans, finely chopped
½ cup butter, melted

Mix graham cracker crumbs, sugar, nuts and butter, reserving 3 tablespoons for topping. Press remainder into bottom and sides of buttered 9-inch springform pan.

2 8-ounce packages cream cheese, softened
1 cup sugar
5 egg yolks
2 cups sour cream
1 teaspoon vanilla
1 tablespoon lemon juice
½ teaspoon lemon rind, grated
½ teaspoon orange rind, grated
5 egg whites

Combine cream cheese and sugar and mix well. Add egg yolks and beat until smooth and light. Add sour cream, vanilla, lemon juice, lemon and orange rind and blend thoroughly. Beat egg whites until stiff but not dry. Fold into cheese mixture. Turn into springform pan. Bake in a 300° oven for 1 hour. Turn off heat and leave cake in oven for 1 hour more. Cool and remove from pan.

Cherry Sauce
¾ cups sugar
2 tablespoons cornstarch
   Dash of salt
⅓ cup water
4 cups frozen, unsweetened, pitted tart red cherries, thawed
3-4 drops red food coloring, if desired

To make Cherry Sauce, combine sugar, cornstarch, salt and water in a medium saucepan. Add cherries, cook and stir over medium heat until mixture begins to thicken. Add red food coloring if desired. Cook and stir for 1 minute more. Chill without stirring. When cool, spoon on top of cheesecake and sprinkle with remaining crumb mixture.

CROCKETT, one of the oldest towns in Texas, is located on a segment of highway that was designated El Camino Real by the King of Spain in 1689. The town is named for Colonel Davy Crockett, and it is believed that he and a small band of men camped there while on their way to join in the defense of the Alamo.

Chocolate Anniversary Cake

This tender chocolate pound cake is perfect for any special occasion.

Serves 12

1 cup butter	½ teaspoon salt
1 cup shortening	½ teaspoon baking powder
3 cups sugar	5 tablespoons cocoa
5 eggs	1 cup milk
3 cups sifted flour	1 tablespoon vanilla

Cream together butter, shortening and sugar. Add eggs one at a time, beating after each addition. Sift together flour, salt, baking powder and cocoa. Add dry ingredients alternately with milk and vanilla, beating after each addition. Grease and flour bottom of a 10-inch tube pan. Pour batter into pan and bake at 325° for 1½ hours or until done. This cake does not need a glaze or frosting, but Chocolate Gloss is wonderful with it.

Chocolate Gloss

½ cup sugar	½ teaspoon salt
1½ tablespoons cornstarch	½ cup boiling water
1 1-ounce square unsweetened chocolate, grated	1½ tablespoons butter
	½ teaspoon vanilla

Mix sugar, cornstarch, chocolate and salt in small saucepan. Add water and cook, stirring constantly, over medium heat until mixture thickens. Remove from heat, add butter and vanilla, and spread on cake while still warm.

Sweets and Treats

TRADITIONAL RECIPES are often interwoven with family and Texas history. This recipe originated with Mrs. J. B. Gillett, wife of Captain J. B. Gillett, illustrious Texas Ranger and early City Marshal of El Paso. It was served at the Christmas dinner interrupted by the news that Pancho Villa had just raided a neighbor's ranch. Mrs. Gillett, a confirmed teetotaler, baked this as one large cake, wrapped it in cloth, and doused it liberally and frequently with whiskey while the cake mellowed. Few in the family ever suspected what gave the cake its wonderful aroma.

Gillett Family Fruitcake

Yields approximately 10 pounds

3 pounds seedless raisins
2 pounds pecans, chopped
2 pounds almonds, chopped
½ pound candied pineapple
¼ pound candied cherries
1 pound dates, chopped
4 cups flour
1 pound butter
1 pound sugar

1 dozen eggs
1 teaspoon mace
1 teaspoon cinnamon
1 teaspoon allspice
1 teaspoon soda
1 tablespoon hot water
1 cup molasses
1 pint peach or apple brandy
   or grape juice

Dredge fruit and nuts in 2 cups flour; set aside. Cream butter and sugar together, add eggs and mix well. Add mace, cinnamon and allspice. Dissolve soda in hot water and stir into molasses. Combine molasses mixture with sugar mixture. Add fruit and nut mixture with the remaining flour. Stir in brandy or grape juice. Bake in 2 large or several small greased loaf pans at 275° for 4 hours or until done.

Make several weeks before serving. Wrap in cloth moistened with bourbon; add more bourbon as needed.

Sweets and Treats

THE "CACTUS JACK" FESTIVAL in Uvalde honors the colorful John Nance Garner, whose long political career took him from the Texas Legislature to the office of Vice-President of the United States. Elected to the Vice-Presidency in 1932 after having been the powerful and influential Speaker of the House of Representatives, Garner commented that it was the only demotion he ever had.

John Garner Cake

*O. C. Fisher, who served more than three decades as United States Congressman from West Texas, is a noted historian and author. His biography of John Nance Garner, **Cactus Jack**, is based on a long relationship as both colleague and friend of the former Vice-President. Mr. Fisher sent us this recipe, which was originally published in the "Progressive Farmer."*

Serves 12

1 pound raisins
½ cup shortening
2 cups sugar
2 teaspoons ground cinnamon
½ teaspoon ground cloves
2 cups boiling water
½ cup hot water
2 teaspoons soda
3¾ cups sifted flour
Dash of salt

Boil raisins, shortening, sugar, cinnamon, cloves and 2 cups boiling water for 10 minutes. Let cool, then add ½ cup hot water with soda dissolved in it. Sift together flour and salt and add to mixture. Bake in a greased 10x6-inch loaf pan at 275° for 1½ hours, or until done.

Sweets and Treats

THE HUMMINGBIRD is the smallest of all birds and a favorite with bird-watchers and casual nature-lovers. Iridescent, all species have needle-like bills to slip deep into flowers. Although their wings appear to be gauzelike, it's the rapid motion that creates the illusion. Most western hummingbird species have been spotted as far east as the Central Gulf Coast. The ruby-throated species is seen in the eastern two-thirds of the state.

Hummingbird Cake

This wonderful, moist cake is a classic throughout the South.

Serves 12

3 cups all-purpose flour
2 cups sugar
1 teaspoon salt
1 teaspoon soda
1 teaspoon ground cinnamon
3 eggs, beaten
1½ cups salad oil
1½ teaspoons vanilla extract
1 8-ounce can crushed pineapple, undrained
1 cup pecans, chopped
2 cups bananas, mashed

Combine the dry ingredients in a large bowl. Mix eggs and salad oil together and stir into dry ingredients. Do not beat. Stir in remaining ingredients until well mixed. Spoon batter into 3 oiled and floured 9-inch cake pans.

Bake at 350° for 25-30 minutes or until cake tests done. Allow cakes to cool in pans for 10 minutes after removing from the oven. Remove from pan and cool completely. Frost with Cream Cheese Frosting.

Cream Cheese Frosting

2 8-ounce packages cream cheese, softened
1 cup butter, softened
2 16-ounce boxes powdered sugar
1 cup pecans
2 teaspoons vanilla

Combine cream cheese and butter and mix together until smooth. Add powdered sugar and beat until light and fluffy. Add vanilla and mix. Spread frosting between layers and on top and sides of cake. Sprinkle with pecans.

Sweets and Treats

SPACE SUITS worn by astronauts, rocks brought back from the moon and continuous shows about man's exploration of space are part of the Lyndon B. Johnson Space Center in Houston. The nearby and incredible Mission Control Center, where much of America's space program originates, offers a glimpse of what is possible in the future of space exploration.

Waldorf Red Cake

Serves 12-16

½ cup shortening
1½ cups sugar
2 eggs
2 tablespoons cocoa
2 ounces red food coloring
1 cup buttermilk
1 teaspoon salt
2¼ cups cake flour,
   sifted before measuring
1 teaspoon vanilla
1 teaspoon baking soda
1 teaspoon vinegar

Frosting
3 tablespoons flour
1 cup milk
1 cup sugar
1 cup margarine
1 teaspoon vanilla

Cream together shortening, sugar and eggs. Make a paste of food coloring and cocoa. Add paste to creamed mixture and mix. Add buttermilk alternately with salt, flour and vanilla. Mix thoroughly. Combine soda and vinegar in a small bowl and add foaming mixture to rest of cake mixture. Pour into 2 greased and floured 9-inch layer cake pans. Bake at 350° for 30 minutes.

For frosting, make a smooth paste with flour and milk and cook over medium heat until thick. Allow to cool. Cream sugar, margarine and vanilla until fluffy. Add to cooled mixture, and blend. Spread over cooled cake.

Mimi's Toffee Crunch

A treasured tradition at Christmas.

Yields 1 pound

1 cup butter
1 cup sugar
2 tablespoons water
½ cup sliced almonds or
   chopped pecans
6 thin milk chocolate bars

Melt butter in heavy, medium saucepan. Add sugar and stir until dissolved. Add water and cook, stirring often, until mixture reaches 290°. Pour into a 12x9-inch pan that has been buttered and sprinkled with ¼ cup nuts. Lay chocolate bars on top of hot candy; spread when chocolate is melted. Sprinkle remaining nuts over chocolate. When cool, break into pieces.

Dulce de Nuez

These pralines are particularly good after you've eaten Mexican food.

Yields 4 dozen pralines

2 cups sugar
1 cup milk
2 tablespoons butter
2 tablespoons white corn syrup
½ teaspoon baking soda
1 cup pecans, chopped
1 teaspoon vanilla

Combine sugar, milk, butter, corn syrup and soda in large, heavy saucepan. Bring to a boil, lower heat and add pecans. Cook and stir until mixture reaches soft-ball stage (328°). Remove from heat and add vanilla. Beat with a wooden spoon until mixture begins to thicken. Drop by spoonfuls onto wax paper. When cool, store in airtight container.

Aunt Jessie's Ice Box Cookies

The Cedar Hall Restaurant in Winkelmann, near Brenham, offers the atmosphere and elegance of the Old South in an authentic 1850's plantation house. High ceilings, chandeliers and antique furnishings make dining in Cedar Hall an experience from the past.

Yields 12 dozen

1½ cups butter
1 cup white sugar
1 cup brown sugar
3 eggs
5 cups self-rising flour
1½ teaspoons cinnamon
½ teaspoon vanilla
2 cups nuts, chopped

Cream butter and sugars in a large mixing bowl; add eggs and mix well. Sift flour and cinnamon into butter mixture and stir until blended. Add vanilla and nuts and mix thoroughly with hands. Shape into 2½-inch rolls, wrap in foil and freeze. To bake, thaw roll slightly, cut into ¼-inch slices and place on an ungreased cookie sheet. Bake at 350° for 5-8 minutes.

Butterscotch Bars

Yields 24 bars

1 cup butter, softened
1 cup brown sugar
1 egg, separated
1 teaspoon vanilla
½ teaspoon salt
2 cups flour
½ cup pecans, finely chopped

Cream butter and sugar in large mixing bowl. Add egg yolk and vanilla. Combine salt and flour, add to sugar mixture and stir until blended. Spread dough in a 13x9-inch pan. Dip fingertips into unbeaten egg white and smooth top of cookie dough. Use only as much as needed. Sprinkle pecans over top and press lightly into dough. Bake at 300° for 40 minutes.

Helen's Coconut-Oatmeal Cookies

Yields 5½ dozen

½ cup sugar
½ cup brown sugar
½ cup butter or margarine, softened
½ cup salad oil
1 egg
1 teaspoon vanilla
2¼ cups flour
½ teaspoon salt
½ teaspoon soda
½ teaspoon cream of tartar
½ cup flaked coconut
½ cup crushed cornflakes
¾ cup uncooked oats
½ cup chopped pecans

Mix sugars, butter, oil, egg and vanilla. Cream well. Sift together flour, salt, soda and cream of tartar. Add to creamed mixture. Stir in coconut, cornflakes, oats and pecans. Shape into 1-inch balls and place on a greased cookie sheet. Flatten with fork. Bake 12-15 minutes at 350°. Do not overbake.

Carmen's Mexican Wedding Cookies

This rich, buttery cookie is a traditional Mexican shortbread popular with everyone.

Yields 2 dozen

1 cup margarine
½ cup powdered sugar, sifted
2 cups flour, sifted
1 teaspoon vanilla
⅓ cup walnuts or pecans, finely chopped
   Powdered sugar

Cream together margarine and powdered sugar. Add flour, vanilla and nuts and mix well. Shape dough into walnut-sized balls. Place on an oiled cookie sheet and bake at 350° for 15 minutes or until they begin to brown. Cool for 5 minutes and roll in powdered sugar.

NEVER MIND those jokes. The Aggies from Texas A&M University are out to save the world—from starving, anyway—with recent high-protein innovations like edible cottonseed, coconut and peanut powders and high-lysine sorghum. Giant vegetables, more tender beef, fireless jalapeños—leave it to the Aggies. This is the brave new world of food technology.

Joyce's Peanut Butter Sticks

These are good for a snack, an appetizer, or to put on a tray of cookies for those who prefer something that isn't sweet.

Yields 40 sticks

20 slices firm sandwich bread
 1 cup creamy peanut butter
 1 cup peanut or corn oil

Cut the crusts from bread and set aside. Cut each slice into 4 fingers. Arrange fingers and crusts on two large cookie sheets and bake at 250° for 50 minutes or until they are very crisp and begin to turn a delicate brown. Cool. Make fine bread crumbs by crushing crusts with a rolling pin or in a blender. Crumbs should have the consistency of cornmeal.

Mix peanut butter and oil until smooth. Dip bread fingers into the peanut butter mixture, shake off excess and roll in bread crumbs. If stored in airtight container, they will keep 2-3 weeks.

Sweets and Treats

MOLASSES IS MORE than just slow. Only since World War II has it ceased to be a major component in the Texas diet. Rich in calcium and protein, molasses is made from sorghum cane, a major crop in Texas. Cornbread and molasses, topped with bacon grease, was once a daily dish for millions. Mixed with sulphur, molasses was a popular tonic. And when it turned sour or sugary, molasses made a good mortar for adobe bricks.

Grandma Collins' Peppernuts

This old fashioned molasses cookie recipe comes from Grandma Collins' family in Wylie. They claim this 89-year-old lady is one of the best cooks anywhere.

Yields 7 dozen

½ cup shortening
1 cup sorghum or molasses
1½ cups sugar
½ cup sour cream
½ cup buttermilk
1 rounded teaspoon baking soda
1 teaspoon cinnamon
½ teaspoon ground cloves
1 teaspoon nutmeg
½ teaspoon ginger
4-5 cups flour

Mix shortening, sorghum or molasses and sugar in a small saucepan and boil for 1 minute. Cool slightly. Add sour cream and buttermilk. Mix soda and spices together and sift with 4 cups flour into molasses mixture. Mix well. If needed, add more flour to make a stiff dough. Chill for several hours.

Remove from refrigerator and form into 1½-inch rolls. Chill again. Slice in ½-inch chunks and bake on a greased cookie sheet for 12 minutes at 350°.

Blue Ribbon Sugar Cookies

These are the best sugar cookies we've tasted and they keep beautifully if stored in an airtight container.

Yields 5 dozen cookies

½ pound margarine
1 cup granulated sugar
1 cup confectioners sugar
1 cup cooking oil
2 eggs

1 teaspoon vanilla
4 cups flour
1 teaspoon soda
1 teaspoon cream of tartar

Cream margarine, sugars and oil until well blended. Add eggs and vanilla and mix. Sift 2 cups of flour with soda and cream of tartar and add to egg mixture. Stir in remaining 2 cups of flour. Mix well. Refrigerate 4 hours or more. When ready to bake, shape dough into walnut-sized balls. Place on a well-greased cookie sheet 4 inches apart. Flatten dough using a flat-bottomed damp glass dipped in sugar. Bake in a preheated 350° oven 13-15 minutes or until delicately browned.

Pecan Crunchies

The contributor of this recipe says she has never taken these cookies anywhere without people asking for the recipe. The happy surprise is that they are so easy to make.

Yields 5½ dozen cookies

½ 16-ounce box graham crackers
½ pound butter

1 cup dark brown sugar
1 cup pecans, chopped

Lightly oil a jelly roll pan and line with graham crackers. Melt butter in a medium saucepan. Add brown sugar and stir until mixture bubbles vigorously. Add pecans and quickly spread over the graham crackers. Bake at 350° for 10 minutes. Cut along indentations of the crackers, leave in pan and freeze for 1 hour. Do not eliminate freezing because that is what makes these so crunchy.

Sweets and Treats

THE PECAN TREE was so loved by Texas Governor James Hogg that his last request was that a pecan tree be planted at the head of his grave and a walnut tree at the foot and that when these two trees bore, their nuts be given to the people of Texas to plant to make "Texas a land of trees." A few years later, the State Legislature voted to make the beautiful pecan the state tree.

Texas Pecan Bars

These are quick and easy to make and wonderful to eat.

Yields 15 bars

2 tablespoons butter
1 cup brown sugar
5 tablespoons flour
   Dash of soda
1 cup chopped pecans
2 eggs
1 teaspoon vanilla
   Powdered sugar

Melt butter in an 8-inch-square pan in 350° oven. Mix brown sugar, flour, soda and pecans. Beat eggs until frothy in a medium mixing bowl and add vanilla. Stir brown sugar mixture into eggs and carefully pour batter over melted butter. Do not stir. Bake at 350° for 20-25 minutes. Let cool, sprinkle with powdered sugar and cut into bars.

Turtle Squares

How can anyone resist a combination of chocolate, caramels and nuts?

Yields 20 pieces

1   14-ounce package caramels
½   cup milk
½   cup butter, melted
1   box German chocolate cake mix
1   cup pecans, finely chopped
1   12-ounce package chocolate chips

Combine caramels and ¼ cup milk in heavy saucepan. Cook over low heat, stirring constantly, until caramels are melted. Set aside. Combine melted butter, dry cake mix, nuts, remaining ¼ cup milk and mix. Press half of dough into a greased 13x9-inch pan. Bake at 325° for 6 minutes.

Take out of oven and sprinkle chocolate chips on top. Spread caramel mixture over chocolate chips. Press remaining cake mixture over caramel. Return to oven and bake 15-18 minutes at 325°. Cool and cut into squares.

Lizzie Ann's Apricot Dainties

Lizzie Ann's Tearoom in Sherman serves these delectable bites on its special party trays. Lizzie Ann's is part of the Houston Street Emporium, a renovated boarding house filled with antiques and shops.

Yields 6 dozen

2   cups sugar
1   cup water
1   pound dried apricots
½   pound pecan halves
    Sugar

Place sugar and water in 2-quart saucepan and bring to a boil over medium heat. Add apricots and boil 7 minutes, stirring frequently. Drain and cover to retain heat. Work with a few apricots at a time so they stay warm and flexible. Fold apricots around the pecan halves to cover, lightly roll in extra sugar and cool. These will keep several weeks if stored in an airtight container.

Sweets and Treats

GILLESPIE COUNTY, in the heart of the Hill Country, is known for the luscious peaches available at roadside stands from late May until summer's end. Iron rich soil and the moderate temperatures make for the tastiest peach in Texas. The women of Fredericksburg, Stonewall and Johnson City make delectable peach pies, cobblers, jams, ice cream and a virtual cookbook full of peachy concoctions.

Gillespie County Peach Ice Cream

Talk about memories of summer!

Yields approximately 6 quarts

6 eggs
1 13-ounce can evaporated milk
2 cups sugar
1 tablespon vanilla
4 cups ripe peaches, mashed
    Milk to fill can to desired level

Beat eggs until light and fluffly. Add evaporated milk, sugar and vanilla and mix until sugar is dissolved. Pour into a 6-quart freezer can, add peaches and fill can with milk to within 4 inches of the top. Freeze according to freezer instructions.

Brandied Peaches

A dessert for the middle of the summer when the freestone peaches are available.

Serves 8

4 large fresh peaches
6 dry almond macaroons, crushed
4 teaspoons brown sugar
4 teaspoons butter
8 teaspoons brandy

Peel and halve peaches; remove stones. Use a teaspoon to slightly enlarge peach hollow. Fill with crushed macaroons. Place ½ teaspoon of both brown sugar and butter in each half. Bake for 20 minutes. Add 1 teaspoon brandy to each half and bake another 20 minutes. Serve cool.

Raspberry Ice with Fresh Peaches

This flavor combination is so good that you'll find it a memorable way to end a summer meal.

Serves 6-8

2   10-ounce packages frozen
    raspberries
½   cup sugar
⅔   cup water
2   teaspoons lemon peel, grated
2   tablespoons lemon juice
2   tablespoons Grand Marnier or
    Triple Sec
6   fresh peaches, sliced
    Mint leaves

Thaw raspberries and push through sieve to remove seeds. Combine sugar, water and lemon peel in a small saucepan. Boil 1 minute; cool. Mix cooled syrup with sieved raspberries and juice, lemon juice and liqueur. Pour into a freezer-proof bowl and freeze 6 hours.

To serve, place a scoop of Raspberry Ice in a glass bowl, surround with peach slices and garnish with mint leaves.

Lemon Sherbet

To enjoy this recipe to the fullest, share with good friends on a hot summer night under those big, bright Texas stars.

Yields approximately 1 gallon

Juice of 8 lemons
Grated rind of 3 lemons
3   cups sugar
2   quarts homogenized milk

Combine ingredients in 1-gallon ice cream freezer container and mix well. Freeze until firm, following instructions that come with your ice cream freezer.

VAST HERDS of wild mustangs roamed the grasslands of early Texas. These small, hardy horses descended from those brought to the region by Spanish explorers; they later escaped from or were abandoned by their owners. As herds increased, Indians and early settlers devised ingenious ways of capturing the mustangs for both food and transportation.

Wild Mustang Grape Pie

The mustang grape grows wild in many areas of Texas. To be used in this tasty pie, the grapes must be picked while the seeds are very small and soft.

Serves 7

4 cups green mustang grapes
2 cups sugar
4 tablespoons flour
½ teaspoon cinnamon
¼ pound butter
¼ cup cream
Pastry for a 2-crust 9-inch pie

Place grapes in large saucepan with enough water to barely cover. Simmer over low heat until they begin to pop open. Mix sugar, flour and cinnamon together and sprinkle half of dry mixture in bottom of unbaked pie shell. Pour cooked grapes, with juice, into shell. Sprinkle remaining dry mixture over grapes. Pour cream over all and dot with butter. Cover with top crust and bake at 350° for 45 minutes or until golden.

Sweets and Treats

SONG PLAYED an important role in the life of the Texas cowboy. Some trail drivers wouldn't hire a cowboy 'lessen he could sing—it didn't much matter if he couldn't carry a tune inside a corked jug; and if he didn't know the words, he could just hum along. Singing had a soothing effect on even the orneriest of Longhorn steers. Cowboys sang "The Texas Lullaby" to head off stampedes and "Nearer My God To Thee" to quiet the herd down at night. Boisterous ballads took over by day, keeping the cowboys entertained and prodding the plodders along. "Old Chisholm Trail" was the most popular: "Come along boys, and listen to my tale. I'll tell you of my troubles on the old Chisholm Trail . . .".

Dispensamé Cobbler

This combination of rich biscuit dough and leftover jams and jellies was a favorite of the cowboys on ranches in the Ft. Davis Mountain area. The name of the recipe means "excuse me," but it may be served for either breakfast or dessert without apology.

Serves 8

2 cups sifted flour
3 teaspoons baking powder
1 teaspoon salt
⅓ cup shortening
¾ cup milk
3 tablespoons butter, soft
1½-2 cups leftover jams and jellies, combined

Sift flour, salt and baking powder together. Cut shortening into flour until mixture resembles coarse meal. Add milk slowly and blend with spoon. Turn dough onto a floured surface and knead lightly. Roll dough ¼-inch thick. Spread with butter and jam and roll up like a jelly roll. Cut into 16 slices, place in muffin cups and bake at 400° for 12-15 minutes.

MIDLAND was so named because it is located halfway between Ft. Worth and El Paso. It is a major oil center and consistently tops the lists of the wealthiest and fastest-growing cities in the United States. The Permian Basin Petroleum Museum in Midland traces the history of petroleum, its production and uses.

Granny's Apricot Pies

The grandmother who is responsible for these little turnovers used to make a dishpan-full as an afternoon snack for her six sons.

Yields 24

Filling

1	pound dried apricots
4½	cups water
5	cups sugar

Pastry

2	cups flour
1	teaspoon salt
1	cup shortening
½	cup water

Mix apricots and water in a medium saucepan. Boil until apricots are tender. Mash and stir until smooth. Add sugar, stir and remove from heat.

To make pastry, mix flour and salt; cut in shortening until mixture resembles coarse cornmeal. Gradually add water and stir until dough is moist. Pinch off walnut-sized pieces and roll out to size of a saucer. Place 1 heaping tablespoon of apricot mixture on half of each circle. Fold other half over and seal edges by pressing with a fork. Prick holes in top of each pie. Place on a cookie sheet and bake at 375° for 20 minutes, or until lightly browned.

Sweets and Treats

PIONEER TEXAS WOMEN took great pride in preparing delicious meals by the ingenious use of the limited ingredients available to them. The Nutt House in Granbury features many such wonderful old recipes. Built in 1893 by Jesse and Jacob Nutt, the Nutt House was a center for social activity in early Hood County. Recently restored, it is located on Granbury's Town Square.

Nutt House Buttermilk Pie

If you have never tasted buttermilk pie, be sure to try this one. It's no wonder people drive a hundred miles for a slice.

Serves 7

½ cup margarine
2 cups sugar
3 eggs
3 tablespoons flour
1 cup buttermilk
   Dash of nutmeg or ½ teaspoon of vanilla or lemon flavoring
1 unbaked 9-inch pie shell

Cream together margarine and sugar. Mix in eggs and flour and beat until fluffy. Fold in buttermilk and nutmeg. For a slightly different taste, you can eliminate nutmeg and add vanilla or lemon flavoring. Pour mixture in pie shell and bake 45-50 minutes at 350°.

Sweets and Treats

OLD-FASHIONED SWIMMING holes in Cypress Creek bring visitors back to the scenic Hill Country area near Wimberley. The shady pools beneath towering cypress trees give way to frothy cascades as the sparkling stream winds and tumbles through the scenic hills. Wimberley, established in 1848, is the gathering place for artists and craftsmen who find the area a quiet retreat from the busyness of the rest of the world.

Cypress Creek Cafe Walnut Raisin Pie

Joanna Johnson of the Cypress Creek Cafe on the square in Wimberley shares this delicious pie with us. The aroma as it bakes is wonderful!

Serves 7-8

1 cup walnuts
1 cup raisins
1 9-inch pie shell, unbaked
5 eggs
1½ cups sugar
¾ teaspoon cinnamon
¾ teaspoon nutmeg
¾ teaspoon allspice
3 tablespoons lemon juice
3 tablespoons milk

Spread walnuts and raisins evenly in bottom of pie shell. Place eggs in medium mixing bowl and beat until frothy. Combine sugar and spices and beat into eggs. Add lemon juice and milk and mix. Pour mixture over walnuts and raisins and bake at 350° for 50 minutes or until center is set. Cool before cutting.

Sweets and Treats

THE PINEY WOODS OF East Texas used to be full of bears and bear tales—like the bear that burned his hand on a pot of boiling meat in a cabin fireplace, then pulled a bottle of liniment off the mantlepiece and doctored himself. Or how about the bear that walked into a country schoolhouse during recess and raided the lunchbuckets, eating only the desserts.

Hattie's Pecan Pie

We tested several superb pecan pie recipes and decided this was our favorite.

Serves 7

4 eggs, slightly beaten
1 cup sugar
1 cup light corn syrup
1 teaspoon vanilla
Dash of salt
3 tablespoons margarine
1½ cups whole pecans
1 9-inch pie shell, unbaked

Mix eggs, sugar, corn syrup, vanilla, salt and margarine together. Stir in pecans and pour into pie shell. Bake at 325° for 50-55 minutes or until filling is almost firm.

French Silk Pie

Serves 7

1½ ounces unsweetened chocolate
½ cup butter
¾ cup sugar
1 teaspoon vanilla
2 eggs
1 9-inch baked pie shell
Whipped cream for garnish

Melt chocolate over hot water; cool. Cream butter and sugar together. Mix in vanilla and chocolate. Add 1 egg and beat with electric mixer for 5 minutes. Add remaining egg and beat another 5 minutes. Pour into pie shell, top with whipped cream and chill.

German Sour Cream Pie

Treasured family recipes are special, and this one comes from Isabel Biehl Horan, who operated the old King's Inn in Kingsville from 1904-1907. Served often at the Inn, this pie is still a family favorite.

Serves 7

1¼ cup sugar
½ teaspoon cinnamon
½ teaspoon nutmeg
½ teaspoon salt
4 tablespoons flour
1 pint sour cream
4 eggs yolks, beaten
3 tablespoons milk
1 teaspoon vanilla
1 9-inch pie shell, baked

Mix sugar, cinnamon, nutmeg, salt and flour together in top of a double boiler. Stir in sour cream. Cook over water, stirring constantly, until mixture thickens. Mix egg yolks and milk. Add small amount of hot mixture to egg mixture, then combine with rest of hot mixture. Cook until thick. Add vanilla, and pour into baked pie crust. Chill for several hours before serving.

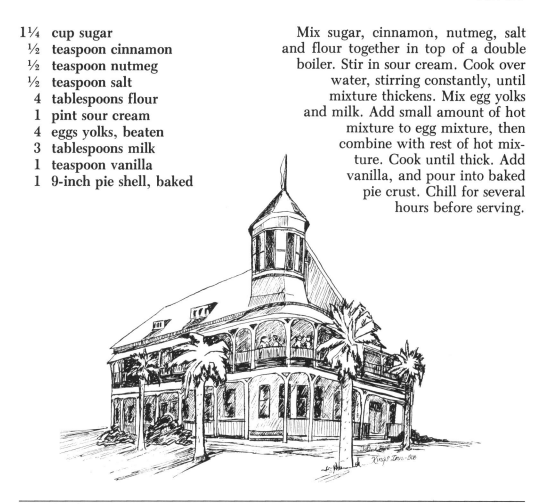

HISTORIC NACOGDOCHES, considered by many to be the oldest city in Texas, served as both the gateway to Texas for settlers coming from other states and as the northern end of El Camino Real, the long road that led south to San Antonio and Mexico. An old legend tells of a great Caddo Indian chief who commanded his two sons to split the tribe and each to start a new village and a new life. One son, Natchitoches, was to take his people, travel three days toward the rising sun and build his village. Nacogdoches, the other son, was to travel three days toward the setting sun and do the same. Today Natchitoches, Louisiana, and Nacogdoches, Texas, sit one hundred miles apart on the sites of old Indian villages.

Nacogdoches Blueberry Dessert

Serves 8

1¼ cup graham cracker crumbs
¼ cup sugar
6 tablespoons butter or margarine, melted
½ cup sugar
1 envelope unflavored gelatin
½ cup cold water
1 cup dairy sour cream
1 8-ounce carton blueberry yogurt
½ teaspoon vanilla
½ cup whipping cream
1 cup fresh or frozen blueberries

Combine cracker crumbs, ¼ cup sugar and melted butter or margarine. Press all but ¼ cup of crumb mixture in 8-inch-square baking dish.

Mix ½ cup sugar, gelatin and water in saucepan. Place over low heat and stir until gelatin and sugar dissolve. Combine sour cream and yogurt and gradually blend into gelatin mixture. Add vanilla. Chill until partially set.

Whip cream until it forms soft peaks; fold in yogurt mixture. Stir in blueberries. Pour into crust. Sprinkle reserved crumbs on top and chill until set.

Sweets and Treats

THE LUSH, PLUMP, BLUSHING strawberries grown in and around Poteet are inspiration for a gigantic Strawberry Festival held every April. More than 150,000 people come to sample strawberry delicacies and to join in all the festivities. The town name Poteet so intrigued comic-strip creator Milton Caniff that he made Steve Canyon's funny-paper niece its namesake.

Poteet Strawberry Meringue Tarts

Yields 12 tarts

1 14-ounce can sweetened condensed milk
¼ cup lemon juice
2 egg yolks, beaten
3 ounces cream cheese, softened
3 tablespoons sugar
1½-2 cups sliced strawberries
12 baked 3-inch tart shells

Blend together condensed milk and lemon juice. Add egg yolks, cream cheese and sugar and beat until smooth. Divide strawberries and place in tart shells. Pour condensed milk mixture over strawberries.

Meringue
2 egg whites
¼ teaspoon salt
4 tablespoons sugar

To make meringue, beat egg whites and salt until white and frothy. Gradually beat in sugar, 1 tablespoon at a time, until stiff and glossy. Spread over filling, sealing to edge of pastry. Bake at 400° for 8-10 minutes or until golden brown.

Variation Filling may be used in a 9-inch baked pastry shell.

Sweets and Treats

THE FIRST COOKBOOK to give ingredient amounts by precise measurements was the *Boston Cooking-School Cook Book* published in 1896. Until then "receipts" would specify "butter as large as an egg" or "three hands full of flour." This may be the reason many of us remember that our grandmothers never measured when they cooked.

Cabinet Pudding

Family traditions give a sense of continuity and become more important as children grow up and establish their own families. For one family, Cabinet Pudding has been its traditional Christmas dessert for nearly a century and is as much a part of Christmas as the wreath hung on the front door.

Serves 12

6 eggs, separated
1 cup sugar
6 tablespoons juice drained from maraschino cherries
1 tablespoon unflavored gelatin
½ cup water
24 almond macaroons, crushed
½ cup maraschino cherries, chopped
1 cup nuts, chopped
2 tablespoons bourbon
Whipped cream, slightly sweetened

Beat egg yolks; add sugar and cherry juice. Soak gelatin in water for 10 minutes. Place egg yolk mixture in a saucepan over medium heat. Add gelatin and water and cook, stirring constantly, until thickened. Remove from heat and cool slightly. Stir in crushed macaroons. Beat egg whites until stiff and fold into macaroon mixture. Add cherries and nuts. Stir in bourbon. Pour into a 13x9-inch glass dish and refrigerate for several hours. To serve, cut into squares and top with whipped cream.

Mocha Nut Freeze

Serves 16

1½ cups graham cracker crumbs
¾ cup sugar
½ cup nuts, chopped
¼ cup butter, melted
1 cup evaporated milk
3 egg whites
    Dash of salt
3 tablespoons cocoa
1 teaspoon instant coffee

Combine cracker crumbs, ¼ cup sugar and nuts in a medium bowl. Add melted butter and mix. Sprinkle 2 cups crumb mixture in buttered 9-inch-square baking dish and press firmly. Freeze. Put evaporated milk in a medium bowl and freeze until ice crystals form around edges of bowl. Beat egg whites and salt until frothy; slowly beat in remaining ½ cup sugar. Whip evaporated milk until stiff and add cocoa and coffee. Fold into meringue. Spread over frozen crumb mixture. Sprinkle with remaining crumb mixture and freeze several hours.

Lemon Lush

Serves 8

½ cup margarine
1 cup flour
1 cup nuts, crushed
8 ounces cream cheese, softened
1 cup confectioners sugar
2 cups whipped topping
2 3¾-ounce packages lemon
    instant pudding mix
2½ cups cold milk

Blend margarine, flour and ½ cup nuts. Press into an ungreased 13x9-inch pan and bake at 350° for 20-25 minutes.

Blend cream cheese, confectioners sugar and 1 cup whipped topping. Spread carefully on cooled crust.

Combine pudding mix and cold milk. Beat until well blended and spread over cheese filling. Gently spread remaining whipped topping over pudding layer. Sprinkle with remaining nuts.

Peach Cobbler Roll

This delicious peach dessert combines the best of a peach cobbler and a pastry roll.

Serves 8

½ cup butter
2 cups sugar (less if fruit is sweet)
2 cups water
1½ cups pre-sifted self-rising flour
½ cup shortening
⅓ cup milk
1 teaspoon cinnamon
2 cups fresh peaches, finely
chopped

Melt butter in 13x9-inch baking dish. Heat sugar and water in medium saucepan until sugar is dissolved.

Cut shortening into flour until mixture resembles cornmeal. Add milk and stir with fork until dough leaves side of bowl. Turn dough onto lightly floured surface or pastry cloth and knead only until smooth. Roll dough out to form a large rectangle about ¼-inch thick. Sprinkle cinnamon over the peaches and spread mixture evenly over dough. Roll dough up like a jelly roll. Dampen edge of dough to seal.

Cut into about 16 slices, and place slices on edge in pan of melted butter. Carefully pour sugar syrup around rolls. (This will look like too much liquid, but crust will absorb it.) Bake at 325° for 35-40 minutes or until most of juice has been absorbed.

Cherry Dreams

This is one of those special desserts that is both pretty and easy.

Serves 8

1 8-ounce package cream cheese, softened
½ cup sugar
½ teaspoon vanilla
1 teaspoon lemon juice
1 8-ounce carton whipped topping
1 21-ounce can cherry pie filling
½ teaspoon almond extract
½ cup slivered almonds, toasted

Combine cream cheese, sugar, vanilla and lemon juice and mix until well blended. Fold in whipped topping. Cover a cookie sheet with waxed paper. Spoon mixture to form 8 individual shells; freeze.

When ready to serve, mix pie filling and almond extract and fill center of each frozen shell. Top with slivered almonds. Chocolate pudding may be substituted for cherry filling.

Cherry Cordials

Chocolate-covered cherries—a delectable goodie to serve with after-dinner coffee!

Yields approximately 18 cherries

½ cup maraschino cherries with stems, drained
½ cup brandy
5 ounces semisweet chocolate

Soak cherries in brandy overnight. Drain brandy and place cherries in freezer. When cherries are frozen, melt chocolate over hot water. Wipe frozen cherries and immediately dip in chocolate. Let excess chocolate drip from cherries, place on waxed paper, and chill.

AN ORANGE brought to a little girl by a missionary priest was probably the beginning of the citrus industry in the Rio Grande Valley. The little girl planted seeds from the orange, and the rich soil and mild climate caused the resulting trees to grow and flourish. The climate of the Valley is tropical, but there have been a few devastating freezes. After each, the citrus growers have come back with better fruit than before.

Mission Oranges with Zest

This is a wonderful light dessert or great addition to a fruit plate.

Serves 8

8 medium oranges
2 cups water
2 cups sugar
½ teaspoon cream of tartar
½ cup Grand Marnier
1 tablespoon grenadine (optional)
½ cup pecans, coarsely chopped

Peel zest from oranges with a potato peeler and cut into thin julienne strips. (Zest is the thin orange outer layer of skin.) Use sharp knife to remove remaining white peel and membrane of the orange so bright orange fruit is exposed. Cut a thin slice from each end of the orange and discard. Slice remaining orange into four fat slices and refrigerate.

Mix sugar, water and cream of tartar in saucepan and add thin strips of orange zest. Cook over medium heat for 25 minutes. Remove from heat, add liqueur and cool. Pour syrup mixture over sliced oranges and refrigerate for at least 3 hours. To serve, spoon into glass dishes and sprinkle chopped pecans on top.

HOUSE SPECIALTIES

From Texas...
with love

Creole Seasoned Salt

A little of this blend of seasonings adds a marvelous touch to beef, lamb, pork, stews and soups.

Yields 1½ cups

¾ cup salt
⅓ cup black pepper
2 tablespoons garlic powder
¼ cup cayenne pepper
2 tablespoons cumin seed
2 tablespoons monosodium glutamate

Mix all ingredients together and store in a tightly sealed jar.

Seasoning Butter

A jar of this stored in the refrigerator is almost as good as money in the bank. The flavor adds a perky touch to vegetables, meats or breads.

Yields ½ cup butter

½ cup butter, softened
2 tablespoons freeze-dried chives
2 tablespoons dill weed
1 clove garlic, finely minced
½ teaspoon salt

Combine butter and seasonings and mix until well blended. Spoon into a small jar and refrigerate for up to 4 weeks.

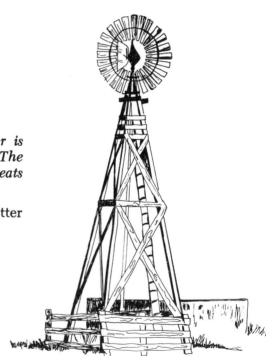

NAKAI BREEN is Cherokee by birth and Kiowa by adoption. Included with her recipes are some special thoughts to share. This is *Nakai's Prayer:* "Great mystery above, when my life is ready to part from mother Earth, please grant me before I go to be able to sit on a high horse and look back at all the paths I have travelled with honor and pride."

Fried Yucca Petals

Nakai says these measurements are approximate, and that the petals taste something like cabbage.

Serves 4

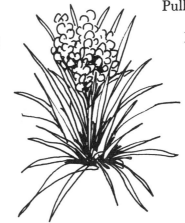

Flower stalk
from yucca plant
1 tablespoon shortening
2 medium onions,
   chopped
2 fresh tomatoes,
   chopped
1 cup water
Salt and pepper
to taste

Pull flower petals from stalk and wash in salt water. Melt shortening in skillet and add flower petals, onion and tomatoes. Stir gently until onions are soft. Add water and simmer until most liquid is gone. Salt and pepper to taste.

I-Ya (Dried Pumpkin Rings)

Slice pumpkin into rings about ½-inch thick. Remove seeds. Place slices on a screen or net and place in a sunny spot for 2-3 days or until dried. These slices may then be stored and kept for stews, soups or puddings.

House Specialties

THE STEAMBOAT-STYLE Nimitz Hotel has been a Fredericksburg landmark for over a hundred years. Captain Charles H. Nimitz came to Fredericksburg in 1847 after leaving the German Merchant Marine. In just a couple of years, the Nimitz Hotel enjoyed a far-flung reputation as the last outpost of civilization between San Antonio and California, a trip of 27 days. Hot baths, wheat bread and sweet butter, fresh vegetables and fruit and beer and wine brewed in the Nimitz cellar were just a few of the comforts offered. Robert E. Lee, U.S. Grant, and Rutherford B. Hayes all signed the Nimitz register. The hotel is now a museum honoring the Captain's grandson, Fleet Admiral Chester W. Nimitz.

Granny Joyce's Pickled Peaches

Jams, jellies and other delicacies with the Granny Joyce label are shipped all over the United States. Most of the peaches canned by Granny Joyce come from the family orchards near Fredericksburg. These peaches are a tasty addition to any meal.

Yields 2 pints

1 cup cider vinegar
1 cup water
2 cups sugar

1 teaspoon ground cloves
1 quart peaches, peeled
6 whole cloves
2 cinnamon sticks

Combine vinegar, water, sugar and ground cloves in a stainless steel pan and boil for 10 minutes. Add peaches to the syrup and cook for 15 minutes or until tender. Pack peaches in 2 pint jars and add cloves and a cinnamon stick to each jar. Fill jars with syrup. Seal and process in a boiling water bath for 20 minutes.

House Specialties

FORT WORTH SPENT a couple of years as Panther City before it became Cow Town. During the 1860's Fort Worth served as a supply depot for northbound cattle drives, and some folks realized that their town could grow into a major cattle shipping center if it only had a railroad. The dream of a railroad faded in the Panic of 1873, and most of Fort Worth moved away. The remaining thousand citizens vowed to fight like "panthers" to get their train. In 1876 they succeeded, and Panther City's claws soon gave way to millions of Cow Town's plodding hooves.

Homemade Chocolate Sauce

Wonderful topping — and easy to do.

Yields 3 cups

2 cups sugar
1 large can evaporated milk
4 squares unsweetened chocolate
½ cup butter
1 teaspoon vanilla
½ teaspoon salt

Boil sugar and evaporated milk in heavy saucepan for 2 minutes. Melt chocolate squares in double boiler and add to milk and sugar. Beat till smooth and add butter. Mix well; add vanilla and salt and stir.

Jezebel Sauce

Yield 1 pint plus

1 10-ounce jar pineapple preserves
1 10-ounce jar apple jelly
1½ tablespoons prepared horseradish
1 1-ounce can dry mustard
½ teaspoon black pepper

Mix all ingredients thoroughly and refrigerate. This sauce is particularly good with ham or cold turkey. It also may be used as an appetizer poured over a block of cream cheese and served with crackers.

Jalapeño Pepper Jelly

Yields 4-5 cups

¾ cup green pepper
⅓ cup jalapeño peppers
5 cups sugar
1 cup white vinegar
1 bottle liquid pectin
2 tablespoons fresh lime juice
Green food coloring, if desired

Seed peppers and chop fine. (Use rubber gloves when handling jalapeños because they contain oils which can be irritating to hands and eyes.) Combine peppers, sugar and vinegar in a large saucepan and bring to a boil. Boil 5-10 minutes. Add pectin and again bring to a boil. Remove, add lime juice and mix. Pour into small, hot, sterilized jars. Seal with melted parafin. Serve with lamb and beef, or spread on crackers with cream cheese.

House Specialties

HISTORIC SAN ANTONIO, home of the Alamo and four other old Spanish missions, is more than a hundred years older than either Dallas or Houston and is considered by many to be the most beautiful city in Texas. The San Antonio River winds through the heart of the city and the beautifully landscaped Paseo del Rio is lined with sidewalk cafes, shops and fountains. Graceful bridges arch the stream, allowing strollers to easily cross to the other side. La Villita, adjoining the riverwalk, is a reconstructed adobe Mexican village filled with shops carrying the products of local artists and craftsmen. The combination of old and new, of Mexican and Texan, of simple and sophisticated, makes San Antonio a unique city.

Eliot's Green Chile Salsa

To add some zing to a hamburger, steak or meat dish, add a little of this special sauce.

Yields 2 cups

3 medium tomatoes, peeled
   and chopped fine
2 fresh green chiles, roasted,
   peeled and chopped fine

⅓ onion, chopped fine
1 tablespoon olive oil
   Juice of 1 lime
1 teaspoon cilantro (optional)

Combine ingredients and
mix thoroughly.

House Specialties

TEXAS GROCERY STORES offer several varieties of chiles in their produce sections. Generally the smaller the pepper, the hotter the flavor. Canned chiles are easy and save considerable time, but the flavor of the fresh chiles is unique and worth the effort. When preparing fresh chiles, use rubber gloves because the pepper oils are irritating to skin and eyes.

Pico de Gallo

This chile sauce adds a special touch to meat tacos or enchiladas, and does wonderful things to a plate of scrambled eggs. Pico de gallo translates "peck of the cock."

Yields 1½ cups

3 fresh long green chiles, roasted, peeled, seeded and chopped
2 green onions, chopped
2 tomatoes, peeled and chopped

2 cloves garlic, minced
1 tablespoon salad oil
2 teaspoons lemon juice
1 tablespoon cilantro, chopped
   Salt to taste

Combine ingredients and refrigerate to blend flavors. This will keep at least 2 weeks in the refrigerator.

House Specialties

TEXAS WINE is the new kid on the block in the wine industry. Most of the 200 vineyards in Texas have been planted within the last few years, and the climate and soil conditions in several areas of Texas have proved ideal for growing grapes. It takes several years for vines to mature enough to produce a wine-making crop; and as they mature, the quality of their yield improves. Local winemakers at the 14 licensed wineries are very determined, and knowledgeable people feel that Texas wines will rival California's within 10 years. So—here's a toast to Texas wines.

Sangria

Serves 6-8

1 orange
1 lemon
½ cup sugar
1 bottle red Texas wine
12 ounces club soda
2 ounces brandy

Slice and seed fruits and place in a large glass pitcher. Add sugar and ½ cup of wine. Use a wooden spoon to stir sugar and press some of the juice from fruit slices. Allow this to ferment at room temperature for several hours. When ready to serve, add remaining wine, club soda and brandy. Stir again. Pour into ice-filled glasses to serve.

Texas Kir

Serves 4

Pour 1 bottle of dry white Texas wine into a large pitcher. Add 5 tablespoons creme de cassis, stir and chill. Serve in large wine glasses filled with cracked ice.

House Specialties

HAVING TROUBLE staying awake? Then perhaps you should try Henry Beckwith's remedy. A legendary south Texas cowboy, Beckwith preferred to work at night so to stay on his toes he drank black coffee laced with the juice of fresh chile peppers. Got a cold? Try this venerable Texas cowboy cure: drink a tumbler full of whiskey mixed with the juice of 100 chile pequin peppers.

Summer Hummer

This good combination is both an after-dinner drink and dessert.

Serves 6

6 ounces coffee liquer
6 ounces rum
3 cups vanilla ice cream

Mix ingredients together until blended. Serve in sherbet glasses.

Yellow Birds

Bring this along for a summer picnic!

Serves 8

1 6-ounce can frozen orange juice
12 ounces canned pineapple juice
12 ounces white rum
6 ounces creme de banana
18 ounces water

Mix all the ingredients in a large glass pitcher. Add a generous amount of ice and serve in your most summery glasses.

TEXAS ONIONS are the sweetest and mildest to be found anywhere. The state is the leading producer of spring onions in the country and No. 2 in total onion production.

Texas Onion Tea Sandwiches

These sandwiches are nippy, but the overnight soak softens the bite.

Yields 84 sandwiches

9 medium onions
3 large green peppers
1 tablespoon sugar
1 teaspoon salt
Water
8 ounces cream cheese, softened
1 cup mayonnaise
Worcestershire sauce and
salt to taste
2 loaves white bread,
thinly sliced
Butter or margarine

Peel onion, and remove seeds and veins from green peppers. Grind together or chop very fine. Place mixture in glass bowl; add sugar, salt and water to cover. Refrigerate overnight.

Drain through clean cloth and wring out well. Place onion mixture in bowl and combine with cream cheese, mayonnaise, Worcestershire and salt.

Cut crusts from bread (if bread is frozen, it will be easier to work with) and save crusts for another day. Butter bread and spread with onion mixture. Top with another bread slice. Cut each sandwich into thirds. Cover with damp cloth and refrigerate until ready to serve.

Texas Sun Tea

The amount of iced tea consumed by the average Texan in a summer month is enormous—and so are the glasses used for serving tea. Sun tea has an especially good flavor and color.

3 family-sized tea bags
3 quarts cold water

Place tea bags in a 1-gallon glass jar and add cold water. Cap loosely and place in a sunny spot for 3 hours. Remove bags. Serve in large ice-filled glasses and garnish with lemon slices or sprigs of mint.

EVERYTHING'S BIGGER in Texas, including its feeds. Governor W. Lee "Pappy" O'Daniel set a record in 1941 when he invited all Texans to attend an inaugural dinner honoring his second term. When 20,000 guests showed up at the governor's mansion, surrounding grounds and streets were converted into dining rooms. Diners tucked away 19,000 pounds of barbecue, 1,000 pounds of potato salad, 1,300 pounds of pickles and onions each, and 32,000 cups of coffee. Actually, O'Daniel had it easy in '41—some 60,000 takers answered the invitation to the first inaugural picnic held in 1939 at UT's Memorial Stadium.

Thomas Earl's Bar-B-Que Sauce

The next time you have Texas-sized barbecue and need a recipe big enough for a crowd, remember this one from Thomas Earl's Restaurant in Arlington.

Yields approximately 2½ gallons

2 gallons catsup
10 ounces Worcestershire sauce
2 tablespoons Tabasco sauce
½ cup white vinegar
1½ cups lemon juice
1 cup prepared mustard

1½ cups liquid smoke
2 tablespoons black pepper
½ cup chili powder
4 garlic cloves, chopped fine
2 quarts water

Combine all ingredients in large kettle and mix thoroughly. Cover and cook over low heat for 1 hour. Do not boil.

Zucchini Relish

This is one of the best relishes I have ever tasted.

Yields 7½ pints

6 large zucchini squash, washed
4 large onions
1 red pepper, seeded
½ cup salt
3 cups plus 1 tablespoon sugar
2 cups vinegar
½ cup water
2 teaspoons celery seed
1½ teaspoons tumeric

Slice zucchini lengthwise and seed by running tip of spoon down center. Put vegetables through medium grind of food chopper. Place chopped vegetables in large bowl, add salt and cover with ice water for 1 hour. Drain, rinse with cold water and squeeze out moisture. Set aside. Combine sugar, vinegar, water, celery seed and tumeric in a large kettle. Bring to a boil and simmer for 3 minutes. Add vegetables and cook 15 minutes or until clear. Seal in hot, sterilized jars.

Pickled Okra

Yields 4 pints

2 pounds small okra
4 cloves garlic, peeled
4 small hot red peppers
4 sprigs fresh dill
4 cups white vinegar
1 cup water
6 tablespoons salt
1 tablespoon celery seed

Wash okra and scrub with a brush to remove fuzz. Pack into 4 sterilized pint jars. Place 1 clove garlic, 1 hot pepper and 1 sprig dill in each jar. Combine remaining ingredients in a medium saucepan and bring to a boil. Pour over okra. Seal jars. Let stand 1 month before serving.

INDEX

Tales

Contributors

Our very special thanks go to the following great Texas cooks, inns and restaurants who, by sharing their wonderful recipes, made the writing of *Tastes and Tales From Texas . . . With Love* a real pleasure.

Garry Able .... Converse
Colleen Albury .... Harlingen
Joyce Andrews .... Houston
The Badu House .... Llano
Phyllis Barker .... Houston
Alma Bassett .... Harlingen
Larry Bennett .... Houston
Decimae Beene .... Friona
Sally Bettiga .... Corpus Christi
Nakai Breen .... Brackettville
Bob and Mary Breunig .... Dallas
Captain "Brownie" Brown .. Rockport
Brushy Creek Inn .... Round Rock
Dennis & Candy Burdette . Carrollton
Patty Carney .... Richardson
Cedar Hall Restaurant .. Winkelmann
Cheese Chalet .... Lampasas
Teddi Cherry .... Rowlett
Wanda Clinton .... Lakeway
Marjorie Cluck .... Austin
Confederate Air Force ...... Harlingen
Convict Hill Restaurant ...... Oak Hill
Carmen Cortez .... Oak Hill
Eleanor G. Cotton .... El Paso
Peggy Cox .... Fredericksburg
Ada Crager .... Canyon
Karen Crager .... Alief
Judy Crawford .... Houston

Gretna Curry .... Midland
Cypress Creek Cafe .... Wimberley
Janet Haig Desjardins .... Houston
Jeanette Donaldson .... Fayetteville
Beverly Dorsey .... Lakeway
Argen Draper .... Hereford
Sally Ellis .... San Antonio
El Paso Chile Company .... El Paso
Hellen Estill .... Temple
Pansy Gillett Espy .... Fort Davis
Ann B. Ethridge .... Beaumont
Pattye Evans .... Houston
L. T. Felty .... Waxahachie
O. C. Fisher .... Junction
Sammi Franklin .... Poteet
Amy Goldson .... Sinton
Reynol Gray .... Austin
Mrs. George Gummelt ... Hallettsville
Patricia Horan Hafey .... Kingsville
Dorine Hagar .... Lakeway
Freda Hamic .... Lampasas
Marjorie Hensley .... Midland
Rebecca Higgins .... Arlington
Ruby Hilburn .... Denison
Pat Holness .... Austin
Jo Ann Horton .... Houston
Institute of Texan Cultures
.... San Antonio

Contributors Cont'd

Loraine McNeil Jackson . Marble Falls
Lois Jacobi .... Dallas
Corinne Jacobson .... Comfort
Dauphen Johnson ....
Joanna Johnson .... Wimberley
Lady Bird Johnson .... Johnson City
Dorothy Kayser .... Snyder
Beverly Kee .... Sinton
Lyn Kerr .... Austin
Norma Kerr .... El Paso
Gayle Kuykendall .... San Antonio
Pam LaShelle .... Round Rock
Dorothy Lawrence .... Tyler
Kathey Leewright .... Whitehouse
Wilda Letbetter .... Brownwood
Lickskillet Inn .... Fayetteville
Lizzie Ann's Tearoom .... Sherman
Fay Keim .... Denison
Manuel's Cafe y Bar .... Austin
Linda Martin .... Athens
Charley McQueen .... Lubbock
Mrs. Charles C. Miller .... Snyder
Jill Miller .... Nacogdoches
Jack R. McGuire .... San Antonio
Robert L. Moore .... Spring
Estela Munoz .... Del Rio
Mrs. James Murchison .... Crockett
Elizabeth Nabers .... Sherman
JoRene Newton .... Kingsville
Nutt House Hotel .... Granbury
Shirley O'Connor .... Lakeway
Debbie Orman .... Lakeway

Joyce Pennick .... Johnson City
Dorothy Polasek .... West
Edwin "Goose" Ramey .... Dimmitt
Monica Reichenberger. Galveston
Merry Rife .... Austin
Claudine Ropka .... San Antonio
Ann Ruff .... Llano
Melina Schubert .... Seguin
Daisy S. Taylor .... San Marcos
Thomas Earl's Restaurant .. Arlington
Texas Peanut Producer's Board
.... Gorman
Rena Tinlin .... Richardson
Elaine Touchstone .. Dripping Springs
Marynelle Tucker .... San Angelo
Beverly K. Tudor .... Port Neches
Bertie Varner .... Kerrville
Bonnie J. Varner .... Lakeway
Rudela Watts .... Luling
Martha Wehling .... Austin
Agnes Weide .... Austin
Mary Werkentine .... Wylie
Whitehead Memorial Museum
.... Del Rio
Ray Winkelmann .... Winkelmann
Adeline Wieczorek .... Dallas
Sybal Woolston .... Garland
Yacht Club .... Port Isabel
Y.O. Ranch .... Kerrville

OUR SPECIAL THANKS TO:

Institute of Texan Cultures, for permission to use two
recipes from their cookbook, *The Melting Pot*
JoRene Newton, for use of her sketch of the Old King's
Inn in Kingsville
Progressive Farmer, Inc., for permission to reprint the
John Garner Cake recipe, Copyrighted © 1961
Ann Ruff, for use of the sketch of the Badu House
Ray Winkelmann, Cedar Hall Restaurant, Winkelmann
Y.O. Ranch, Kerrville, for reproduction of their brand

SPECIAL SOURCES OF RECIPES:

The Badu House, Llano
Cedar Hall Restaurant, Winkelmann
Cheese Chalet, Lampasas
Convict Hill Restaurant, Oak Hill
The Culinarian, Monica Reichenberger, Galveston
Cypress Creek Cafe, Wimberley
The El Paso Chile Company, El Paso
Granny Joyce's, Fredericksburg
The Inn at Brushy Creek, Round Rock
Lizzie Ann's Tearoom, Sherman
Lickskillet Inn, Fayetteville
Manuel's Restaurant, Austin
Nutt House, Granbury
Texas Department of Agriculture, Austin
Texas Peanut Producer's Board, Gorman
Thomas Earl's Restaurant, Arlington
Y.O. Ranch, Kerrville

Notes

Notes

If you would like to order additional copies of this book, or if you enjoyed this book and would like to order one of the other books written by Peg Hein, we have included an order blank below.

Name of Book	Price	Postage & Handling	Quanity
Tastes & Tales From Texas...With Love	14.00	2.25	_____
MORE Tastes & Tales from Texas	14.00	2.25	_____
New Tastes of Texas (Low fat Tx. cooking)	14.00	2.25	_____
Life's Too Short Not to Live It As a Texan	8.00	1.50	_____

Texas residents should add $1.05 sales tax for each cookbook and 60 cents sales tax for *Life's Too Short Not To Live It As a Texan.*

Heinco, Inc.
101 Explorer Cove
Austin, Texas 78734
Phone: (512) 261-6085

My check is enclosed for the books indicated above. Please send them to:

Name_____

Address_____

City_____ZipCode_____